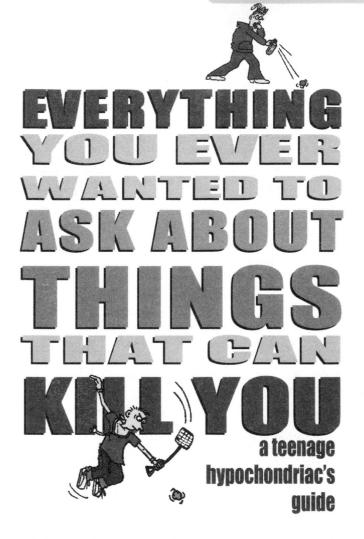

# EVERYTHING YOU EVER WANTED TO ASK ABOUT THINGS THAT CAN KILL YOU

### a teenage hypochondriac's guide

**Tricia Kreitman and Dr Rosemary Jones**

**Illustrations by Kathryn Lamb**

Piccadilly Press · London

*To our children*

First published in Great Britain in 2005
by Piccadilly Press Ltd,
5 Castle Road, London NW1 8PR

A catalogue record for this book is available from the British Library

ISBN: 1 85340 699 6 (trade paperback)

1 3 5 7 9 10 8 6 4 2

Printed and bound in Great Britain by Bookmarque Ltd.
Design by Louise Millar
Cover design by Fielding Design

Set in Legacy and Stumbeleina

# EVERYTHING YOU EVER WANTED TO ASK ABOUT THINGS THAT CAN KILL YOU

**Tricia Kreitman** worked as a psychologist, designing sex education programmes for young people, and then as a psychosexual therapist before becoming a full-time author and broadcaster. She has been an advice columnist for eighteen years, specialising in young people's and women's problems, and she is currently working with the BBC World Service. A parent of teenagers herself, Tricia was a director and then Chair of Brook Advisory Centres for young people for six years. She is also an experienced TV and radio broadcaster. Tricia has published widely in the general medical and lay press.

**Rosemary Jones** is a consultant paediatrician from Bath. In addition to specialising in young people's health, she works with children with autism and children who are living apart from their birth families. She combines her career with hands-on experience with young people – she has seven children, aged fourteen to twenty-four.

# Contents

# Acknowledgements

It would have been impossible to write this book without the generous help and support of many people. Our heartfelt thanks go to: all the young people who entrusted us with their stories – we have changed names and identifying details where necessary, but we hope you approve of the end result; John Coleman at the Trust for the Study of Adolescence for his enthusiasm and encouragement; Samaritans and the Suzy Lamplugh Trust for their generosity in allowing us to include some of their brilliant advice; Dr Adam Bradford, who gave us an insight into the GP's view of teenage problems; and Karen Amos for her good-humoured and never-ending patience and support.

Thank you all.

# How to Use This Book

- You may choose to read this book all the way through or just dip into one or more sections that are of special interest to you.

- Each chapter starts with an overview of its contents. You can also look up specific diseases in the index at the back.

- Chapter 9 is an emergency tool kit of information and practical advice for coping with accidents and emergencies anywhere you may be.

- Chapter 10 looks at ways of getting further help and advice and some of the factors that cause people to worry in silence rather than to ask for the support they need.

- The Contacts section lists a wide range of support services and helplines.

- The Glossary explains many of the medical words you may come across in the different chapters.

# Introduction

Why write a book for young people about things that can kill you? It's a pretty morbid subject – particularly when you consider that teenagers are less likely to die than any other age group in the population. However, both Rosemary (a consultant paediatrician specialising in adolescent health) and I (a psychologist and advice columnist) know from our own work and our years of research together that death *is* an issue for young people – and that there *is* a need for user-friendly information on things that can kill you. These are the reasons why:

Firstly, although the chances of young people dying are low, the causes of death in young people are different from the causes in earlier childhood and later life. Did you know that the top three causes of death in young people are 1. accident and injury, 2. suicide and 3. cancer? The tragedy is that many of these deaths are preventable, yet the early warning signs – e.g. risk-taking behaviour, depression and the early symptoms of cancer – often go unrecognised.

Secondly, our own research with young people shows that, along with the more obvious worries about relationships, body image and bullying, etc., fear of death – either their own or the death of someone close to them – is a major anxiety. When questioned, older teenagers often told us how, several years previously, they had worried in silence for weeks or even months over puzzling symptoms they had thought must have been due to some fatal disease. Yet they had rarely felt able to ask a family member or medical professional for advice.

Our third and final reason for writing this book is to challenge the modern taboo around the subject of death. Although it affects everyone in our society, people still find it very hard to talk about death and dying. That reluctance is then passed on to and picked up by young people.

So this book is mostly about things that are unlikely to be a danger to you – but which will be even less of a danger when you know more about them. We've also included some facts about other illnesses that might affect you or someone close to you.

Our aim is to help you:

- be aware of warning signals and potential dangers;
- be able to take emergency action when necessary;
- know how to get help for yourself or a friend when it's needed.

With luck, you will never be faced with any of these situations, but if the unexpected does happen we want you to have a better chance of getting through it in one piece!

– TRICIA KREITMAN

# Statistics About Death in Children and Young People

Compared with other age groups, young people are much less likely to die or get a serious illness. Nevertheless, some young people *do* die, and the table on page 5 shows the most common causes of death. In some cases there is nothing anyone can do to prevent an illness or death, but in other situations it is more likely that someone can be cured if they have their problem diagnosed early. That's why it's so important to be aware of the warning signs of serious diseases so you can ask for help or advice as soon as you are worried. Remember, any doctor would far rather be able to reassure you that nothing was wrong than think that you were waiting and worrying in silence.

Most of the statistics about illnesses and causes of death are given as numbers per million of the population. The figures shown on the opposite page are provided by the Department of Health, and are for the year 2002. They refer to deaths in England and Wales.

The table is divided into two columns, showing the numbers of young people aged five to fourteen and fifteen to twenty-four who died from various causes. In each box the numbers are shown for males (m) and females (f).

## Deaths Per Million of the Population in 2002

| Deaths caused by: | 5–14 years | 15–24 years |
|---|---|---|
| Total deaths (all causes) | (m) 139 (f) 136 | (m) 633 (f) 254 |
| Accidents and suicide | (m) 32 (f) 15 | (m) 237 (f) 55 |
| Cancer | (m) 38 (f) 27 | (m) 59 (f) 41 |
| Infections, e.g. meningitis, lung infections, blood infections | (m) 4 (f) 4 | (m) 7 (f) 9 |
| Diseases of the heart or blood vessels – usually problems you are born with | (m) 7 (f) 6 | (m) 32 (f) 24 |
| Lung diseases, such as asthma and some lung diseases you are born with | (m) 9 (f) 9 | (m) 17 (f) 12 |

More detailed statistics are available and are provided on individual causes of death. These are grouped in different age ranges – for children under one, between one and four, five and nine, ten and fourteen, and for young people aged fifteen to nineteen. Similarly, the adult statistics cover each five-year age range. So later on in the book, you will see tables looking at death rates for the age groups ten to fourteen and fifteen to nineteen.

Much of the other data in the book has been taken from *Key Data on Adolescence*, which is published by the Trust for the Study of Adolescence.

# 1 Death – What Do We Know About It?

**This chapter covers:**

- What *Don't* We Know About Death?
- What Happens to the Body at the Moment of Death?
- How Does a Doctor Test for Death?
- What Happens to the Body After It Has Been Taken Away?
- What Is a Post-Mortem?
- What Should I Expect if I Go to See a Dead Body?
- Funeral Customs
- The Grieving Process
- Helping Someone Who Is Grieving

The real aim of this book is to help you avoid the most common causes of death in young people. However, we have to be honest from the start and admit that – sooner or later – everyone dies. Yet talking about death has become a major taboo in our society, and people don't like even *thinking* about it if they can help it! But it wasn't always like this. When someone died fifty years ago, the family would probably have kept the body at home, maybe in the dead person's own bed, while friends and relations came to 'pay their respects'. This usually meant spending a short time sitting beside the body, often alone, talking and privately saying goodbye to someone you cared for. Even quite small children were encouraged to do this.

Today, this is rare and many people go through most of their lives without ever having seen a dead body. When someone dies at home or in an accident or in hospital, the body is often whisked away and may not be seen again by even the close family until it has been enclosed in a coffin ready for burial or cremation. This is because people in our modern, Western culture feel uncomfortable with the thought of death. We are horrified that, despite all out amazing science and technology, we still can't control the inevitable. We also often have a fear of overwhelming emotions. Expressing anxiety for someone who is dangerously ill or grieving over a death can feel like a loss of dignity – and control. Parents may also try to protect their children from these emotions by keeping information from them about their own or another family member's illness.

It's normal to become more aware of death during your teenage years. We know from our research that many young people worry about their own death or losing someone close to them. It's also at this age that many people find themselves attending a funeral for the first time. You may have questions about dying and death that are difficult to ask anyone close to you for fear of upsetting them at a time when they're already grieving for someone they've lost. You may even feel embarrassed or guilty for having these questions, but curiosity is normal and, hopefully, the rest of this chapter will provide some guidance for you.

## What *Don't* We Know About Death?

We might as well admit now that we don't have an answer to the really big question, i.e. what happens to us after death? Every religion and culture has its own ideas on this. Of course, it's not knowing that can make death so frightening. If you have a religious faith that promises life after death, then you might not fear death – or the loss of those close to you – as much as other people.

Even those without faith often hope that there is something good after death, particularly when a close friend or relative dies. It's very common for a bereaved person to imagine that they hear the footsteps or even the voice of the person they've lost or to think they've caught sight of them in a crowd. You may also feel that the person who has died is somehow close to you, watching you and caring for you. Whether this is evidence of a spirit world or afterlife – or simply wishful thinking – it is comforting and reassuring. And it can help take some of the pain out of the long process of grieving. However, perhaps the most important thing we can do for the dead is remember them. At first this may be difficult without sadness and tears, but remembering them and talking to friends and family about all the times you shared together will help keep them alive in your mind. Funerals, celebrations of remembrance and other gatherings of family and friends play a big role in this, providing support for the living as well as a way of sharing memories of the dead.

## What Happens to the Body at the Moment of Death?

Whether someone has been in an accident, has suffered from a long illness or dies from old age, the ultimate cause of death is usually the fact that the heart stops beating. The heart is a pump that drives blood around the body. The blood carries fresh oxygen breathed in through the lungs to be used as fuel by every different part of the body. When the heart stops beating, the blood stops flowing so there is no more fuel available. The brain usually survives for a few minutes longer until it is starved of oxygen and closes itself down. At this point the person has died.

In some cases the heart can be helped to beat for longer,

keeping the person alive. For example, an important part of first-aid tuition is resuscitation, or cardiopulmonary resuscitation (CPR). This simple but life-saving technique allows you to breathe air into someone's lungs and press on their chest in a regular rhythm to do the job of the heart for a short while. Many, many people's lives have been saved in this way because they were kept alive until medical help arrived.

## How Does a Doctor Test for Death?

A doctor will check the 'vital signs'. They will first of all feel for a pulse, probably by putting their fingers on the person's neck. They will look and listen for signs of breathing and then use a stethoscope to listen to the chest for up to a minute to establish that there is no heartbeat. The doctor may then shine a torch into the patient's eyes to check whether the pupils still react to light. If the person is dead, the pupils will remain large and black, even when a torch is shone directly into them.

Because the heart has stopped pumping blood, a body will start to look unnaturally pale within a couple of minutes of death. After about an hour, other signs appear, including the breaking up of tiny blood vessels in the back of the eye (something that can only be seen by a doctor using an instrument called an ophthalmoscope). After several hours, the muscles in the dead body start to change and release enzymes (natural chemicals) which cause the muscles to become very stiff. This is called rigor mortis and it lasts for about twenty-four hours, during which time it is very difficult to alter the position of a body.

# What Happens to the Body After It Has Been Taken Away?

When someone dies at home, a doctor will be called to confirm the death and then the relatives usually call an undertaker (sometimes called a funeral director), who will take the body away, often within a few hours. They prefer to do this before rigor mortis sets in, because it's easier to move the body at that point. If someone dies in an accident, the body will be taken to hospital for the death to be confirmed and from there to the hospital's own mortuary – a place for temporarily storing the dead – or to an undertaker.

The undertaker or the hospital staff will then 'lay out' the body. This involves washing it, brushing the hair and dressing it either in the person's own clothes or in a simple white robe. When a body relaxes after death, the bowels and bladder can often leak so cotton wool is packed into the body openings to stop any body fluids flowing out.

# What Is a Post-Mortem?

If a death is unexpected and the person hasn't been seen by a doctor within the last few days before he or she died, UK law says that there has to be a post-mortem (autopsy). This does not usually mean that the authorities are suspicious about the cause of death; it is because it is important to understand why someone has died, and sometimes that knowledge can be very useful.

A post-mortem involves opening up the body to check on the state of all the organs and examine any disease or injury. Obviously this is a very unpleasant thought, but it's often comforting for the family to know exactly what caused the death and it may also help others. For example, some diseases can be passed on in families, and knowing about them in advance can often save or prolong other people's lives.

## What Should I Expect if I Go to See a Dead Body?

Relatives are often relieved at how peaceful and happy the dead person looks if and when they go to view the body at a funeral home. Even if there has been a post-mortem, everything will be stitched back together and the stitches will be hidden under the clothing. The undertaker may have applied some light make-up to the face to try to give it a natural colour. Because any pain that the person may have felt before death has gone and the facial muscles are relaxed, they look at peace and, with their eyes closed, almost as though they are sleeping.

It can be a very daunting experience visiting a dead body but, if it's someone close to you, you may feel better having seen it. The reality is often much less frightening than what you may have been imagining. You may want to say a few words out loud or quietly inside your head. You may even want to touch their face or hand to say goodbye. The body will feel cold, but you won't do them any harm. However, if you don't feel comfortable seeing or touching the body, you should tell your family. Just say that you would prefer to remember the person as they were when they were alive.

## Funeral Customs

Different cultures and religions deal with death in different ways. The body may be buried or cremated, either with a full religious funeral service or just a gathering of family and close friends to say goodbye. If someone knows they are dying, they may choose to think about and plan their own funeral by writing it down or talking it through with people close to them before it happens. But when somebody dies suddenly, particularly when they're very young, the choices have to be made by those who are still alive, often parents and immediate family. The choices they make and the arrangements that are made will try to reflect something of the person who has died, but also attempt to comfort the living.

One thing that's common in many religions is for there to be a gathering after a funeral where family and friends can eat and drink together and talk about their memories – both happy and sad. If you've never been to one of these events, it can feel a bit strange because you may find that people are smiling and laughing and catching up on gossip and family news. It doesn't mean they aren't sad, but getting together in this way provides a release of tension after a funeral and offers an opportunity to laugh at funny memories, to remember the good times together and to show support to the bereaved family. It's one of the first stages in the grieving process and the beginning of a roller coaster of emotions that can last for years.

## Tom's Story

I had a friend at school whose mum was dying of cancer. Although we never said anything, we all thought it was really weird that he'd talked to her about dying and even planned her funeral with her. Then, last year, one of my best friends was killed in an accident. There was no warning, and we were all in shock, and the funeral and everything happened really quickly. Then his parents asked us if we would help plan a memorial service. They said they wanted all his friends to remember him the way he really was and, as we were close to him in a different way from them, we could help by suggesting things that he would have liked. Four of us got together and came up with some suggestions. We read bits out of some of his books and played some of his favourite music. We even told some jokes, because he always did! It was hard to do, and I almost broke down, but it really seemed to help – not just me but everyone else as well.

*Tom, 17*

# The Grieving Process

The grieving process, or mourning, is the process of coming to terms with a death and slowly letting go of the person you loved. It is like an emotional journey with no set path. No one can tell you how to do it, but it can be comforting to know that there are certain common stages that most people will find themselves at at some point.

**Numbness:** This often happens immediately after a death and may be your mind's way of protecting you from the shock. Often, the first few days after a death are very busy. Arrangements have to be made, friends and family come to visit to give support and the phone rings all the time with calls from people who have just heard the news. Onlookers may say how well you're coping, while you just feel distant and removed as though you've been switched over to automatic pilot.

**Denial:** At one level you know the person has died but at another you're still expecting them to walk into the room. You may try to convince yourself that it is all a mistake – and any minute now someone is going to come in and tell you that everything is all right. You might feel that it's simply impossible for this person to be dead because you loved them so much.

**Anger:** You may feel angry and furious with the world in general or with God in particular for taking away someone you loved. If the death was the result of an accident, you may look for someone to blame. Some people take their anger out on close family and friends, making life very hard for everyone around them, but usually it's a phase that passes, so try to be patient and understanding.

**Depression:** As the reality of the loss sinks in, you may become very depressed and withdrawn. This is a dangerous period and, just when you really need help, you may be incapable of asking for it. That's why it's so important that friends and family support and look out for people who have been bereaved, encouraging them to get help when it's appropriate. The depression may also bring on unpleasant symptoms like panic attacks or may weaken your immune system, leaving you more vulnerable to illness.

**Acceptance:** This is the beginning of the new part of your life. Nothing will ever be the same again, but you are able to start to think about the person you've lost without overwhelming and crippling pain. At this stage a bereaved person often starts making positive plans again for themselves or their family. Until now it may have been impossible to consider anything hopeful or enjoyable about the future.

Throughout all this, your emotions go up and down and all over the place. You may feel very guilty for having survived when someone else has died or for having said bad things – or not having said more good things – to them when they were alive. You may also become very anxious about your own health or just short-tempered and lacking in patience with anyone around you. It can be very hard to keep up with school work or other interests, and you may feel isolated from your friends when they can't understand why you don't seem to be the same person any more. Make an effort to explain to your closest friends how you are feeling. It may not be easy, but it will help them to help you. No one can pretend that grieving is easy, but talking about and sharing your feelings can help. If you don't have people close to you that you feel comfortable to do that with, there are many other ways of getting support. See the Contacts section at the end of the book for ideas.

## Helping Someone Who Is Grieving

If you are the friend watching someone you care for trying to cope with the pain of bereavement, it can feel very difficult to know how to help. You may be reluctant to ask questions – even simple ones like 'how are you?' – for fear of reminding them and causing even more pain. Try to remember that there is no danger of 'reminding' them of their loss – because there's no way they could forget! But they may be feeling cut off from you and the rest of the world because of their grief. Showing that you can share that and aren't afraid of the strength of their emotions can be a great help. Don't be embarrassed if their pain also moves you to tears – crying together can be surprisingly supportive. If you can't speak to them or feel too shy to say how you feel, try writing a letter or sending a card to tell them that you are thinking of them.

Practical help is also very important. Offering to share notes of missed lessons at school or keeping in touch about some joint project can help on a day-to-day basis. And just offering to spend time together – going for a walk, watching a DVD or listening to them try to make sense of what has happened – can also be a tremendous comfort.

Be patient and be aware that there may be bad days when your friend is angry, moody or reluctant to see you. If necessary, back off – but call back the next day to show that you do care and are still there for them.

## Susie's Story

I was seventeen when my mother died and just about to take my final exams at school. She'd been ill for a while with cancer, and I knew it was coming, but I still had no idea how I would feel. After she died people were tiptoeing around me and I wanted to say, 'I'm all right', but I couldn't, and I realise now I probably wasn't anyway. I'll always remember that one of our neighbours did something very kind but really unexpected. She came round a couple of days after my mum's death with a book, a novel. She said, 'I know you probably don't feel like reading this, but it's important you take some time off from grief. Don't feel guilty for not feeling sad all the time. No one expects you to behave in any special way.' She was right. I didn't feel like reading anything at all, but I took it upstairs and the next thing I knew two hours had gone by. Everything was still just as awful, but I had managed to step outside the grief and my misery for a short while and, because of what she said, I didn't feel guilty. It was a long time ago now, but I can still remember that book and I'll always be grateful for her kindness.

Susie (a long time later)

## Emma's Story

I was really, really close to my nan, and when she died I missed her so much. I had visited her in hospital a lot, and when Mum and Dad asked me if I wanted to go to the funeral I said of course I did. I even helped to plan it and make sure we played some of her favourite songs. But the next day, when everybody had gone home, it was like nothing had happened. Everyone was sad and everything, but nobody mentioned her. I hated it and I tried to say things, but every time I started to talk about her my mum looked so upset that I backed off. But then I just felt worse and worse and was crying myself to sleep most nights. A few weeks later I was round at my friend's house and her mum asked me how I was getting on. She knew about my nan, and I found myself telling her how I felt. She explained that my mum was also probably trying not to upset me, but that both of us would feel better if we could talk about our feelings and our memories. I went home and told Mum that I really missed Nan and wanted to talk about her with someone who loved her as much as I did. We both cried, but we talked and we laughed as well, and after that everything seemed to be a lot easier.

*Emma, 15*

# 2 Accidental Death

**This chapter covers:**

- The Total Number of Young People Who Died in 2002 and the Number of Deaths Caused by Accident, Suicide and Self-Harm
- The Main Causes of Accidental Death
- The Effects of Peer Pressure
- The Effects of Alcohol
- Driving and Risk-Taking
- Accidental Drowning
- Accidental Poisoning
- Violent Crime

Most young people are healthy and their chances of dying from anything at all are extremely low. However, people aged fifteen to twenty-four are more likely to die of an accident than at any other time in their lives. It is therefore not surprising that accidents are the major cause of death in young people. The second-largest cause of death is suicide. Sometimes it is difficult to separate out the statistics for accidental death and suicide because doctors and coroners are often reluctant to record a young person's death as being due to suicide or deliberate self-harm because this is so upsetting for the family. Instead, an inquest may return a verdict of 'accidental death'.

Our figures are taken from government statistics for England and Wales.

### The Total Number of Young People Who Died in 2002 and the Number of Deaths Caused by Accident, Suicide and Self-Harm

| Age | 10–14 years | 15–19 years |
|---|---|---|
| Total deaths (all causes) | (m) 280 (f) 189 | (m) 833 (f) 384 |
| Deaths due to accident, suicide and deliberate self-harm (including 'cries for help' that went wrong) | (m) 76 (f) 31 | (m) 396 (f) 107 |

You can see from this table that accidents, suicide and deliberate self-harm account for a large proportion of the total deaths in these age groups. In the next age group up, those aged nineteen to twenty-four, the figures are even higher.

You can also see that the risk for boys at all ages is higher – and for the fifteen to twenty-four age group it is more than four times greater than it is for girls. This is mainly due to the fact that boys tend to take more risks and that boys are also more likely to commit suicide.

The main cause of accidental death is traffic accidents – involving young people as drivers, passengers and pedestrians.

### The Main Causes of Accidental Death

| Age | 10–14 years | 15–19 years |
|---|---|---|
| Pedestrians killed in a traffic accidents | (m) 19 (f) 8 | (m) 30 (f) 10 |
| Cyclists killed in traffic accidents | (m) 9 (f) 4 | (m) 9 (f) 0 |
| Motorcyclists killed in traffic accidents | (m) 2 (f) 0 | (m) 45 (f) 4 |
| Car drivers or passengers killed in traffic accidents | (m) 8 (f) 10 | (m) 156 (f) 56 |
| Accidental drowning | (m) 4 (f) 2 | (m) 10 (f) 0 |
| Killed following an assault | (m) 2 (f) 2 | (m) 18 (f) 9 |

Accidents happen for various reasons. However, some factors make young people more vulnerable to accidental death. Knowing – and thinking – a bit more about these might just help keep you safe!

## The Effects of Peer Pressure

Peer pressure is when a person makes a decision or changes their attitude, response or behaviour in order not to be different from the people around them. People often talk about peer pressure as something that only happens to young people. Forget it! Peer pressure is everywhere. It's just that parents sometimes conveniently forget that they often follow the crowd just as much as their kids do.

Peer pressure isn't always a bad thing; sometimes the majority, i.e. the crowd, really does know what's right! And, usually, you have to get your ideas and opinions from somewhere, so it makes sense to listen to what other people say – and then make up your own mind. Ask yourself every so often whether what you think is your choice genuinely is an informed and independent decision – make sure you are not blindly following the crowd.

When it comes to talking about accidents and risk-taking, peer pressure is a very active force.

### Examples of Peer Pressure

- Taking up smoking because everyone else is doing it.
- Drinking until you throw up because your friends say that's the only way to prove you've had a good time.
- Standing by or even joining in when someone gets bullied because you don't want the attention to turn on you instead.
- Accepting a lift home in a car when you know the driver is way over the drinking limit because no one else seems to mind – and you don't want to be left on your own.
- Going out with an older person you may not feel very safe with just because you and your friends think he's really attractive.
- Reading the same newspaper for years on end because it's what friends, parents, etc., read.
- Jury or committee members changing their opinion so they don't have to carry on arguing with the rest of the group.
- Countries going to war because their larger and more powerful allies tell them it's the right thing to do.

### How to Stand Up to Peer Pressure

Many (if not most) people find this very difficult to do. Others delight in questioning everything before deciding for themselves. This approach isn't always easy, convenient or popular, but it does gain you a certain reputation – either as an individual freethinker and potential leader or someone who's downright difficult!

On a practical level, you could try these steps:

- Be aware of the influence of drink, drugs, etc. Would you even be considering doing this if your head was clear?
- Ask questions all the time: first of yourself, then of others. If people look uncomfortable or don't seem to want to answer your questions, the chances are you've hit on a problem they'd rather not face. That's usually a warning sign.
- See if you can find a way of compromising – when you know an idea is wrong but there's absolutely no way of persuading others to change their mind completely.
- Look for others who are expressing doubt or trying to stand up against the group. Maybe they have a point. Be prepared to find out more and back them up if necessary.

## The Effects of Alcohol

Accidents, suicide and violence are major causes of death in young people. Alcohol is often involved in all three. The following facts speak for themselves:

- One in six people who go to hospital Accident and Emergency (A & E) departments have alcohol-related injuries or problems.
- After eleven p.m. in busy A & E departments as many as seven out of ten people are there because of the effects of alcohol.
- One in seven people killed on the roads is involved in drink-driving accidents.
- Although the number of young people who die directly due to the poisonous effects of alcohol is quite small (between ten and twenty per year), the number of 'years of life lost' due to alcohol is huge. Alcohol contributes to about half of all cases of people who die younger than they would be expected to die.

- More than 6,000 young people under the age of sixteen are admitted to hospital each year because of the effects of alcohol or drugs.
- About 1,000 of these people need emergency treatment to save their lives.
- Alcohol poisoning occurs more quickly in children and young adults – they get low blood-sugar levels, become cold and develop breathing problems more quickly than an older person who has drunk the same amount.
- Almost one in six young adults – aged sixteen to twenty-four – is dependent on alcohol.

## Alcohol and Driving

Most young people are pretty sensible about not drinking and driving. Although you are 'allowed' to drive after drinking a small amount of alcohol, the best advice is not to drink and drive at all. It is really difficult to stop after one drink if everyone around you is carrying on, so try to decide in advance if you are likely to want to drink – and, if so, leave the car at home.

You may not realise that lots of drunken pedestrians are involved in accidents every day – in fact, half of the young people who are killed by cars while they are crossing the road would have failed a breath test themselves. It is also very dangerous to cycle while drunk.

## Alcohol and Violence

Some people get very aggressive when they have been drinking and are much more likely to start a fight in which they, and others, could get badly hurt. The problem with alcohol is that it relaxes you to start with, but that effect doesn't last long. Also, people who have drunk alcohol are more susceptible to group pressure and are easily encouraged to do something reckless.

Some facts:

- Almost half of all young people who are injured or assaulted say that the incident was committed by someone who was drunk.
- When young offenders – who have been arrested for a crime – go to court, about one in four say that they were drunk when they committed the crime.
- One in four young people say that they have damaged or destroyed something after drinking.

## James's Story

James and his two mates from university, Ali and Mike, decided to treat themselves to a long weekend on the south coast after their exams. One night they stayed up having a few drinks in a bar, sitting outside because it was still hot even at two a.m. Some local students turned up, completely drunk, weaving about all over the pavement. They started laughing and pointing at Mike, saying: 'Are you gay? Come here, gay boy, and give us a kiss.' Mike tried to ignore them, but they came up and started to push him in the ribs and grab his cheeks and squeeze them. His mates got up and asked the students to go away and leave them alone. The next thing they knew there was glass flying everywhere, Mike had a bleeding cut on his face, and James was lying on the ground with two of the students taking it in turns to stamp on his head.

Ali managed to run inside the bar, and in a few seconds the police arrived and arrested the other boys. Mike and James spent the next three days in hospital, having scans and checks and getting their wounds stitched up. For the first two days, the doctors weren't sure whether James might end up blind in one eye. Meanwhile, Ali spent hours and hours in the police station trying to get everything sorted out. On the third day the students turned up at the hospital practically in tears. They were incredibly apologetic and sorry for what they had done, saying they had never gone out and got so drunk before. One of them was a medical student, and the other two were hoping to be lawyers. Mike and James were surprised to find that, despite the fact that these boys had nearly killed them, they had a lot in common! All three boys were shocked that people who could be really nice when sober changed so completely when they were drunk. And, as a result, they have all cut down on their own drinking.

### Alcohol and Sex

Another risk of getting drunk is that you may make different decisions from the ones you would make if you were sober. Lots of young people have sex with someone for the first time when they are drunk – and many feel pretty awful about it afterwards. Often, they completely forget about contraception or sleep with someone they don't really like very much – or hardly know.

Some facts:

- Among younger teenagers, those aged thirteen to fourteen, as many as forty per cent of those who had sex said afterwards that they were drunk or 'stoned' – on drugs – at the time.
- About one in seven girls say that they have had sex when they were drunk and have later regretted it.
- Unprotected (and therefore unsafe) sex is far more common when one or both partners have been drinking.

Some people think it is peer group pressure that makes a number of young people drink. This certainly can happen, but it may also be the case that people who are already experimenting a lot with drinking alcohol are likely to choose friends who share the same interests – so groups of drinkers tend to hang around together. In the same way, people who take all sorts of risks – like driving too fast, having sex without contraception, drinking too much or using drugs – are often attracted to others who are doing the same things.

### What to Do if You Are With Someone Who Is Drinking Heavily

This is a difficult situation, but if you find that you are the sober person at a party you do have a responsibility for your mates. They may not welcome your help, but this doesn't mean that you should just abandon them!

In practical terms, this means that if you are with someone who has been drinking heavily and then vomiting, you should try to stop them from going to sleep straight away – by walking them around, preferably in the fresh air, giving them some strong coffee, and keeping them talking. Otherwise they could fall asleep, be sick again and inhale their vomit. If they do fall asleep, then try to put them into the recovery position (see Chapter 9) and check again in ten minutes to see if they can be woken. If they are moving around and complaining when you disturb them, they are probably just drunk and sleepy and bad-tempered, but if they don't respond to you then they may be unconscious and you should call for help.

## Driving and Risk-Taking

You may have just passed your driving test or be starting to plan your lessons and looking forward to some real independence. Learning to drive is the easy part – for most young people, finding the money to pay for car insurance is the real problem. Many insurance companies refuse to insure anyone under twenty-one, and even those who do offer insurance to young people charge huge amounts. There is a simple explanation for this. Your risk of having an accident is higher compared with other age groups, so the insurance company is much more likely to have to pay out money – often for the damage to someone else's car or their medical treatment. The risk which most young people are well aware of is drink-driving. To eliminate the risk, *never* drink any alcohol if you know you will be driving.

### How Can You Cut Down the Risk?

Most accidents happen soon after people pass their test. While they have been learning to drive, they've usually been the only person in the car apart from their instructor or parent. Then, when they have their licence, they start offering lifts to all their friends. It's easy to turn the music up loud, chat away and simply get distracted. Huge numbers of accidents happen at traffic lights – you only have to glance away for a second, the lights change, the person in front puts their brakes on suddenly, and next thing you know you have run into the back of them. You might not have done much damage to your own car, and may think a few more dents don't matter, but whenever you go into the back of someone, legally it is your fault – and the other driver will claim against your insurance. And sometimes people who are quite cautious when they are driving on their own become less cautious when they're with mates or begin to show off – overtaking when they can't quite see if the road is clear, or speeding round a corner. Speed kills – either you or your passengers, or any pedestrians who suddenly run out into the road. Also, remember that even if you are in complete control, another driver may not be so alert.

If you want to cut down your chances of having a crash:

- Spend a few weeks after you pass your test getting used to driving on your own.
- Leave the sound system off at first.
- Stick to the speed limit – it's there for a reason. Either the road isn't safe for high speeds or there are likely to be people around.
- If you are driving a long way, take plenty of breaks.
- Think seriously about having a couple of lessons specifically for driving on a motorway before you go out on one for the first time.
- Think about doing the Advanced Motorist course – not only will you be a better driver, but you'll also get cheaper car insurance.
- Keep your concentration when mates are with you – tell others to keep the noise level down, etc.

If you are offered a lift by someone who has just passed their test, think carefully before you accept, and never ever 'dare' them to go faster or take any risks. It isn't clever – it's just stupid!

Most important of all: don't drink and drive and don't get into a car with a driver who has been drinking.

Here are just a few examples of some stupid things that a group of young drivers told us they had done in the first few weeks after passing their test:

**Jenny** drove from Leeds to Bradford at ten p.m. with no lights on – and although she noticed that other drivers were flashing their lights at her, she didn't have a clue why. By some miracle she got there in one piece – but when she realised what she had done, she spent most of the night awake worrying about what could have happened.

**Chris** was fast asleep in bed at one a.m. when the door bell rang. His friend Vicky had been out to a club, got separated from her friends, had hung around in town for a taxi for half an hour, and had then got into a panic because she knew she was going to be home really late. So she walked round to Chris's to ask him to give her a lift home – she lived in a small village about five miles out of town. He crawled out of bed, drove her back safely, and then on his way home drove straight into a wall, because he didn't notice a sharp bend in the road. Damage: £2,000 repair bill for a car that was worth only £3,000! Luckily, Chris was OK, but he could have been badly injured.

**Hannah** offered her three school friends a lift into town. She knew the route like the back of her hand, but they all got chatting and then started singing really loudly. She suddenly realised she was in the wrong lane at a roundabout, and cut straight across the path of another car to reach her exit. Result: two of the friends had whiplash injuries to their necks and the car was a write-off.

# Accidental Drowning

Although drowning isn't a very common cause of death, it is worth mentioning because it is one of the causes that can be easily avoided if you follow simple rules.

## Paul's Story

Paul and his mates had just finished their end-of-year summer exams, so straight after school arranged to meet up by the weir. Paul was the tallest among his friends, so he popped into the supermarket on the way and stocked up with some vodka and cola. Two of his friends managed to grab some bottles of wine from their parents' fridges, and some of the girls sorted out crisps and nuts. They had a brilliant afternoon, until Paul managed to kick the football into the river. Suddenly, Paul and a couple of his friends found themselves jumping in – still with their heavy jeans on. Paul could not believe how freezing cold the water was – especially as it was a baking-hot summer's day. He was usually a reasonably good swimmer, but it was really hard with his wet jeans pulling him down. He started to panic when he got caught up in weeds at the edge of the river, and the next thing he knew was that he was being dragged by the current over the edge of the weir. His mates thought he was messing about at first, so they simply laughed and cheered from the edge. Luckily, there was a family having a picnic just downstream, and the father managed to wade in and catch Paul as he was tumbling past. He dragged him to the side and helped him climb out – and then gave him an earful for being so stupid!

So before you go for a swim, take a few simple precautions:

- Never swim anywhere where there are warning signs not to do so – they are there for a good reason. There might be a strong undertow or lots of weeds, which you could get tangled up in.
- Always check how you could get out of the river or lake – it is often all too easy to jump in and then to discover the bank is really slippery or too high above the surface of the water for you to grab hold of.
- Never swim in jeans or other heavy clothes – they will soak up lots of water and drag you down.
- Never, ever swim when you are drunk – your coordination will be awful and your arms and legs will feel weak and floppy.
- Don't jump in just because your mates have all done it – you should know your own limitations. You may be able to swim several lengths of a swimming pool, but swimming in a river takes a lot more energy, especially if there is a strong current

and you have things like squelchy mud at the bottom and poor visibility underwater to deal with.

- Don't dive (or jump) into water you are not familiar with.
- Remember that if the water temperature is really cold, you may die of hypothermia (low body temperature).

SWIMWEAR
(RECOMMENDED)

SWIMWEAR
(NOT RECOMMENDED)

## Accidental Poisoning

Deaths due to accidental poisoning occur mainly in people who experiment with drugs. Sniffing solvents – e.g. glue or aerosols – can cause death almost instantly. Many other young people die when they take a purer form of a drug than they are used to or a mixture of drugs. Often it is the combination of drugs with alcohol that is fatal – the person becomes unconscious and may then stop breathing. There is more information on the specific problems related to different drugs in Chapter 5.

People don't often die as a result of taking too many over-the-counter drugs – those that you can buy from a pharmacist – but they can certainly become quite ill if they don't read the information on the packet. Lots of painkillers are sold under different brand names, and you might think that if you have had a couple of one particular brand of pills and they haven't helped your headache, it will be OK to take a couple of something else. It may not be! Drugs that can cause big problems are paracetamol (which can cause liver failure and death) and codeine – which can make you feel very woozy and light-headed, and can make your heart race. Each packet of painkillers will say how often you should take them – so make sure you look at this, and check the ingredients before you try something new. Some medicines, like cold and flu remedies, also contain a lot of painkillers, so again read the info on the packet.

## Beth's Story

It was my first night at university and after settling into my grotty room in the hall of residence and waving my (weeping) mum goodbye, I summoned up all my courage to knock on the door of the girl in the room next door and suggest we went down to the Student Union bar for a drink. We had a brilliant night in the end, with most of us getting pretty drunk, and ending up in one of the boys' rooms in the corridor next to ours. I remember noticing that Andy, who was going to be on my course, was looking even worse for wear than most of us – his face was a horrible grey/greenish colour and he could hardly stand up. He said he had a splitting headache and took about four painkillers. Soon after that I decided I really had to get some sleep or I'd never make it to registration the next day, so I went back to my room. Although I had the worst ever hangover the next morning, I managed to crawl out of bed and sort out my registration and find my way around the campus. I was totally shocked when I got back to hall that evening, to see that there was a police car and ambulance outside. It turned out that Andy had collapsed in his room and he wasn't found until his roommate, Dave, finally woke up at four in the afternoon. Andy was in a heap on the floor, surrounded by his own vomit, and was as white as a sheet. I couldn't believe it when I found out that he had died – he had inhaled his own vomit, and he was so sleepy because of all the booze mixed with the painkillers that he didn't have the strength to cough and clear the stuff out of his lungs. Dave was so shocked and upset that he gave up his course and went home. The rest of us managed to stay on, but we could never forget what happened.

*Beth, 20*

# Violent Crime

Watching the news or reading the newspapers, it would be easy to assume that violent crime, including murder, rape and mugging, is on the increase. Yet we're safer now than we were ten years ago. The British Crime Survey (BCS) reported that all violent crimes (including rape) had fallen by thirty-six per cent between 1995 and 2004. The BCS is thought to be an accurate measure of actual events because it includes details of unreported crimes, including domestic violence, street fighting, etc., as well as those that are reported to the police.

Other studies have shown that people often have a very realistic idea of the low level of risk in their own lives or neighbourhoods, but assume that things are much more dangerous in other parts of town or other places in the country. The media has to take some of the blame for this because newspapers are well aware that violence and shocking headlines sell extra copies and they often concentrate on scary headlines rather than feel-good stories.

Nevertheless, crime does exist and you are more likely to be a victim of violent crime if you are:

- male,
- aged sixteen to twenty-four, and
- regularly spend time in pubs, wine bars or other places where people are drinking heavily.

In view of the above it is not surprising that the group of people most at risk of violence is young men.

However low the actual crime figures may be, it still makes sense to look out for your personal safety and be aware of any potential risks. These include signs that situations are getting out of control, such as:

- people drinking heavily and becoming abusive;
- fights breaking out;
- a crowd of people splitting into two or more 'gangs';
- the appearance of knives, firearms or other weapons.

In any of these situations you would be sensible to get out of the way – even if the temptation is to become involved or take sides yourself. And it's much easier to think clearly and walk away in a non-aggressive manner when you haven't been drinking too much yourself. You are then in a better position to phone or call for help if necessary.

The Suzy Lamplugh Trust gives excellent advice on all areas of personal safety, and we would strongly recommend looking at their website, *www.suzylamplugh.org.* (See Contacts for further details.) Some of their safety tips are mentioned in Chapter 9.

# 3 Suicide, Depression and Mental Illness

**This chapter covers:**

- Suicide
- What to Do if You Feel Suicidal
- Recommendations from Samaritans
- Depression
- How to Recognise Depression in Yourself or a Friend
- Self-Help for Depression
- Treatments for Depression
- Other Common Mental Health Problems

Research suggests that about twenty per cent of children and young people suffer from some kind of emotional or mental health problem. Of these, about one in three will go on to have problems as an adult.

After accidents, suicide is the second most common cause of death in young people. But the official figures may well be an underestimate. And for every young person who does attempt suicide there are many more who suffer from severe depression, a range of mental illnesses and suicidal thoughts. This chapter looks at how you might recognise these problems in yourself or a friend and suggests ways of getting help and treatment. You might also want to look at Chapter 8 about ways to stay healthy, where there is a section on positive mental health.

# Suicide

## *Facts About Suicide*

- Suicide is the second most common cause of death among young people (after accidental death).
- Each year, twice as many young people (of all ages) die from suicide as from road traffic accidents.
- Young women aged fifteen to nineteen are more likely to attempt suicide than any other group of the population – but they are only a third as likely actually to die from a suicide attempt as young men.
- About a fifth of all the deaths of young people in the UK are due to suicide – and some people suggest that the figure is actually much higher. Any sudden death requires an inquest, and coroners are often unwilling to attribute a young person's death to suicide, classifying it instead as an 'accident' or 'undetermined'.
- Most young people will think about suicide at some point. Seven per cent of thirteen- to eighteen-year-olds report having recent suicidal thoughts.

## *Why Suicide?*

Evidence suggests that most young suicides kill themselves out of a sense of hopelessness. According to MIND, the UK mental health charity, people usually attempt suicide to block out unbearable emotional pain. It may be a cry for help rather than a real determination to die. Someone attempting suicide may be so confused and upset that they are unable to see any other options or choices. Many people considering suicide give out warning signs in the hope that someone will help them. They want to find a way to stop their pain and may take their lives only when there seems to be no other way.

Experts think that young people are particularly at risk from suicide because they are more impulsive and have relatively less life experience. This means that when something bad happens, they tend to see it as permanent and unchangeable rather than as something that they might get over in time. The effects of surging hormones and mood swings common during adolescence can magnify feelings of hopelessness.

Not surprisingly, suicide is strongly linked with depression – it's likely that about seventy per cent of suicides were noticeably depressed before they died. However, other things can also increase the risk of someone attempting to take their own life:

- Drugs and alcohol can increase depression at the same time as reducing inhibition, so someone is more likely to make an impulsive suicide attempt. Some research has suggested that about a third of suicide attempts are made under the influence of alcohol.
- Relationship problems and family break-up.
- Bullying – in or out of school.
- Performance pressure, e.g. to succeed in exams.
- Physical or sexual abuse – either current or in the past.
- Having had a relative or close friend who died through suicide.

Most important of all, ten to fifteen per cent of young people who attempt suicide WILL eventually die by suicide.

These figures are shocking, particularly when you consider that hundreds of young lives could be saved every year if people noticed the warning signs, listened when someone was in pain and were prepared to take action by offering help or suggesting where to get help when it was needed.

## Why Is There a Difference in the Suicide Rates Between Boys and Girls?

In the UK every year, about 19,000 young people make a suicide attempt and, of those, around 700 will actually kill themselves. However, there's a big difference between the sexes. Young women aged fifteen to nineteen are far more likely to attempt suicide, but young men are around three times as likely to 'succeed'. Overall, the suicide rate for young men has doubled in the last twenty years.

Increased use of drugs and alcohol by younger men may contribute to this, but another reason for the difference between the sexes could be that men (of any age) tend to use more violent methods when attempting suicide. They may hang themselves, jump in front of a train, or use firearms or poison if they're available. Compared with, say, taking an overdose, there is much less chance that they will be discovered in time and saved. However, the story probably isn't as simple as that.

Young men are far less likely than young women to go to a GP or any other professional with their mental health problems. They also tend to have less effective support groups among their friends. Women are good at talking about problems and sympathising with each other, but many men find this sort of discussion difficult and uncomfortable – even among close friends.

## Rachel's Story

I was seventeen and in my last year at school when everything started to go wrong. Things had been difficult with my boyfriend for several months; we kept breaking up and getting back together again, but I was terrified of losing him. I was also really worried about my course work and the coming exams. Then one night he came round and said that it would be better if we ended our relationship now. I begged him to reconsider, but all he said was that we'd have to be friends instead. I didn't sleep all night, and my mum knew first thing in the morning that something was wrong. She tried to get me to talk about it, but I wouldn't, and I just went to school hoping that everything would be back to normal. I tried to see him at lunchtime and after school, but he said he was busy and couldn't stop. I rang his mobile all that evening but it was switched off and he didn't return my messages or texts. That night I told my mum that we'd broken up and she was great – but also said she thought it might be for the best because he'd been causing me so much grief.

The next day at school everyone seemed to know about it, and I couldn't bear them feeling sorry for me. Then, even worse, I heard rumours that he already had another girlfriend. Eventually, I asked my best friend Bella whether this was true. She looked really uncomfortable but said that it was and admitted that she'd known for a week or so but hadn't known how to tell me. She was great and came round to my place that night and listened while I went on and on about him. Again I cried all night, and I couldn't face going to school the next day. My mum could see I was in a really bad way, so she agreed that I could take the day off as long as I did some work at home. But, of course, I couldn't concentrate. I couldn't think of anything except him. Then I started to think that there wasn't any point in doing anything anyway. He'd been my life, so why would I want to go on without him? And also, if I was dead, I wouldn't have to feel like this any more.

I hadn't really decided to do anything, but I went to the bathroom cabinet to see what was in it. I found a packet of paracetamol with only a few tablets used from it. I took it downstairs and sat in the kitchen looking at it. One minute it seemed silly and the next it seemed the obvious thing to do. Then I quickly swallowed all the tablets, drank a glass of water, then went up and lay on my bed waiting to see what would happen. I felt a bit odd, but I wasn't sick or anything and I didn't fall asleep, so I assumed I just hadn't taken enough tablets. I looked around the house to see if there was anything else, but I couldn't find anything and, anyhow, I felt calmer now.

I didn't say anything to my mum when she came home, but I did feel that maybe I ought to tell someone what I'd done. I knew I was all right but for a moment I had been thinking about killing myself. Eventually, I rang Bella, but her mum answered. I've known her for years and I don't know whether Bella had told her or whether she could just hear it in my voice, but almost the first thing she said to me was: 'Are you all right?' I just sat on the floor in my bedroom and told her all about it – breaking up with him, feeling that everyone knew but me and not seeing any point in going on. She asked me whether I'd done anything 'stupid'. I asked her what she meant, and she said that she was worried I might try to hurt myself. I felt a bit foolish but admitted that I'd taken some pills at lunchtime. She went very quiet and then asked me to tell her exactly what I'd taken and when. She explained that paracetamol is particularly dangerous because, while a small overdose may not have any immediate effect, it can attack your liver, causing severe problems and even death several days later. I hadn't known this, and I was really shocked. She then said that now that I'd told her she had to do something about it and needed to make sure that my mum knew so I could see a doctor as soon as possible. She guessed I didn't want to tell Mum myself but said she'd do it for me and asked me to put her on the phone. By this time I was really scared, but my mum wasn't angry or anything like I'd expected. She gave me a great big hug and said we'd better get this sorted out, then took me to the casualty department at the local hospital. When she told them what had happened, they saw me straight away and took some blood from my arm to see how far things had gone. Luckily, they said that my blood level of the drug was not at a dangerous level and I didn't have to stay in hospital overnight, but that I had to come back the next day to talk to a psychiatrist.

I wasn't looking forward to that, but he was really nice and understanding. He fixed up some counselling for me and also spoke to the school so that they would lay off the pressure a bit about exams, etc. I wouldn't say everything is fine now, but I do feel there are people who understand and care for me. I can't really believe that I tried to kill myself, but I did mean it at the time. I'm just so glad that I didn't succeed.

*Rachel, 18*

### What to Do if You Feel Suicidal

Everyone gets depressed sometimes and the idea of suicide crosses most people's minds. The most effective thing you can do to help yourself is to talk to someone else. Many people who feel suicidal deliberately avoid talking to friends and family about their feelings. They don't want to upset them, but they may also feel unable to explain their distress adequately and worry no one would understand them.

Being listened to and understood is the first step in getting through this crisis. Not everyone is good at doing this – some people may try to give you answers or tell you to 'pull yourself together'. But if you have someone you can trust to listen and care for you, then contact them – NOW. It might be an old friend, a friend's mum or a teacher at school. Samaritans offer great support for anyone feeling desperate. Their helpline is free, confidential and open twenty-four hours a day, every day of the year. They won't tell you what to do, but they will listen and be totally non-judgemental. See Contacts for details.

### Recommendations From Samaritans*

Samaritans recommend the following to see yourself through periods of stress:

### 1. Don't give yourself a hard time

Don't blame yourself if you're not feeling great. You're not alone.

### 2. Spot the signs of trouble

If the future seems bleak and you've lost interest in everything, you need to sort it. Watch out too for trouble sleeping and eating, drinking too much or being anxious or angry. They're all signs that something's wrong. So if you feel moody, don't give yourself a hard time – take it seriously. And take action.

### 3. Look after yourself

If your body's fit, your mind's more able to cope. So eat sensibly. Get enough sleep. Don't rely on alcohol or drugs to get you through. Take exercise to raise your mood. Take time out for you. And give yourself the occasional treat – you deserve it!

### 4. It's good to talk

Talking your problems through with someone else will help. So don't let your pride stop you getting it sorted. Find someone you trust, who'll keep what you've told them confidential, and let it all out. Unexpressed emotions can stop you coping with everyday life. When you talk about them, you'll find you're thinking more clearly and you're more able to get things sorted.

### 5. Ask for help

Know when you need to get help – and don't be afraid to ask. It's a sign of strength, not weakness. If you want to talk about anything that's bothering you, you can get in touch with Samaritans at any time of the day or night. They won't tell you what to do and won't tell anyone you called. But they will listen for as long as you need.

*Reproduced with kind permission of Samaritans. Copyright free.

# Depression

## *What Is It?*

No one feels happy and outgoing all the time; some people are just better at putting on a performance than others. And everyone has experienced at least a taste of what it feels like to be depressed. It may have been caused by something as simple as a grey winter's day, too much homework or the after-effects of a row with a friend. Some common illnesses like flu can leave you feeling very down and unenthusiastic about life.

Most people bounce back from these lows and, even when they're feeling wretched, have the insight to appreciate that one day, whether it's tomorrow or next week, they'll probably feel a bit better. But sometimes depression can take a tighter hold and you feel that life has totally slipped away from you. It becomes extremely difficult to motivate yourself to do even the most routine things and you may start sleeping a lot or finding it impossible to sleep, overeating or completely losing your appetite and losing all patience and enthusiasm for talking to friends and family.

This type of depression, sometimes called clinical depression, can start in various ways. In many cases it's the response to some type of serious life event, e.g. the death of someone close to you or breaking up with a boy/girlfriend. You feel isolated, cut off from all the normal small pleasures and major excitements of life and, no matter how much everyone tries to cheer you up, you retreat into yourself without seeing any way out of your pain. On the other hand, some people slip or fall into depression without any obvious trigger event. It can feel as though a switch has flipped in your mind and a weight dropped on to your soul. Instead of being brightly coloured and hopeful, your life and the world around you appear grey and flat and hopeless. Severe depression can be linked to an imbalance of brain chemicals or hormonal problems and can also have a genetic basis, so that depression may 'run' in families.

Unfortunately, some adults find it hard to accept that young people get depressed. They come out with the tired old line of 'these are the happiest days of your life' and expect you to pull yourself together. But teenage depression can be very serious. It is frequently a sign of deeper problems and may even lead to a suicide attempt. This type of depression is an illness, and the good news is that it can nearly always be cured, although it may take time and patience. As with many illnesses, the key to getting better is to get help. The catch with depression is that it can make you believe that nothing on earth could help you. So someone suffering from depression may not see the point in getting help. Even if they do, depression can make them feel so lethargic and miserable that they can't make the effort to do anything about it. That's why friends and family are so important in recognising depression and encouraging the sufferer to get the advice and support and, if necessary, treatment they need.

## Different Experiences of Depression

I have suffered from depression on and off for years. Even when things are 'good' I can still feel it there, ready to put its hand on my shoulder and push me back under. It's like a reflection of everything in my real life but sometimes it seems far more real than life, if you see what I mean. Even though I know I've come through it before with help, when the depression hits it seems like there's no way out. I lose my appetite and all I want to do is sleep, but I never feel any better for it.

Jasmine, 19


My mum died when I was twelve. Although I'd known she was very ill, I couldn't believe she'd really left me. People said I was in shock

46

because I couldn't cry, not even at the funeral – but I just felt as though there was a big plastic screen between me and the rest of the world. Sometimes it was like I was even watching myself as well as everyone else. I began to think a lot about what it must be like dying and being dead. Sometimes the only thing that made me feel I really was alive was when I hit or cut myself. I looked at the blood and the bruises and it was as though I was watching my own pain. For once I was feeling and knew that the real me was still there inside. Nothing else seemed to touch me.

*Vicky, 16*

When I was about thirteen and all my friends started talking about girls, I knew I had to shut up and pretend to be like them. Girls to me were only ever going to be friends; it was boys I liked and dreamed about! I knew there was no way I could ever let on that I was gay, so I had to pretend to be somebody else. I felt I was living in a shell and I was sure that someone would find out. I started to imagine that people were trying to catch me out, and I felt that every comment was directed at me. I started to dread going to school and often had headaches or stomach aches on Monday mornings.

*Jon, 17*

## Facts About Depression

- Five per cent or more of teenagers are seriously depressed – but many of these cases go undiagnosed and do not receive help.
- One in three young people feels depressed at least once a week.
- Depression increases the risk of alcohol or drug abuse – BUT drugs and alcohol can make depression worse and raise the risk of suicide.

## Risk Factors

Sometimes there is no obvious trigger to depression, but in many cases an event or change in someone's life seems to start it off. People can respond in very different ways to the same trigger, so although finding yourself in one of these situations doesn't mean that you'll necessarily become depressed, it does raise the risk of it happening:

- changes in family, e.g. parents separating or divorcing – or worry that they might do so;
- having a parent or carer who is depressed or in a state of worry over their own life;
- being bullied;
- being abused – either now or in the past;
- feeling different from everyone else – perhaps because of the way you look, your size or your race;
- serious illness or death of someone close to you;
- arguments with close friends or family;

- having trouble with a boyfriend or girlfriend or the break-up of a relationship;
- moving house away from your friends or leaving home;
- worrying about your sexuality;
- exams or pressure to succeed.

## *How to Recognise Depression in Yourself or a Friend*

As with most illnesses, different people can have different symptoms. Having any of these symptoms doesn't necessarily mean you have a problem, but people who are depressed may:

- feel sad and miserable even in circumstances where they are normally comfortable and happy
- become unusually moody or snappy or irritable, even with close friends and family
- feel lonely and cut off from family and friends
- see no point in doing anything and feel nothing is worth bothering with
- want to stay in bed all the time and sleep far more than is normal for them
- have difficulty sleeping – either finding it hard to fall asleep or waking up during the night or the early hours of the morning
- lie or make up stories about themselves and their family
- steal or behave in a way that attracts trouble
- not feel hungry and lose weight – or start comfort-eating and put on weight
- feel they don't matter to anyone and that no one would miss them if they weren't around
- start to think that no one likes them and that others are talking about them behind their back
- think about ways to harm themselves or show signs of self-harm like cuts, scratches or burns on their arms, legs or body.

If you recognise several of these symptoms in yourself or a friend, then you should consider whether you – or they – are depressed. It can be hard to accept this but, sometimes, knowing that there is a reason for the way you feel can in itself start to make you feel better. If it's a friend you're worrying about, you may find they get angry or resentful if you start asking them questions but, if you care about them, you must try to be understanding. You can't force them to get help but, by showing your concern and suggesting different ways of self-help or places or people they could turn to for advice, you can encourage them.

Look in the Contacts section for helplines, etc. – and remember that you can always call one yourself to ask for advice if you are worried about a friend.

### *Self-Help for Depression*

Even quite severe depression usually gets better after a while – but it can take months or even years. One of the major symptoms of depression is a feeling of hopelessness, that nothing you or anyone else can do will make things better. But, in fact, finding ways to help yourself or getting help from other sources can make life a lot easier and shorten the period of depression. In many cases, simple DIY self-help strategies can bring a big improvement.

For example:

- Depression involves a load of negative feelings and emotions building up inside you. It is really important to find ways to communicate how you feel – even if it seems as if nothing will help you. Talk to someone who will listen and accept what you tell them. A good friend, a parent, a favourite teacher, your doctor or a helpline are all possibilities. See Contacts for more suggestions.

- You could also try painting, drawing or writing about how you feel. Expressing the misery and numbness inside can help shift it.

- Listening to your favourite music or, even better, dancing around the room on your own to it can lift your spirits.

- Any form of exercise will release chemicals into your blood that give you a short natural 'high'. Go for a jog with the dog or go swimming at the local baths. Taking regular exercise will also help you sleep better – and you will feel more rested when you wake up.

- Eating a regular, healthy diet (don't forget breakfast!) and getting a few good nights' sleep can make a difference.

- Watching your favourite video, reading your favourite book or generally doing anything else you normally enjoy can also help. So, even if you don't feel like doing anything, try to make the effort and force yourself.

PAINT YOUR FEELINGS !

## Treatments for Depression

One of the problems with depression in young people is that it often goes unnoticed or undiagnosed. People put it down to 'teenage moods'. Families are tied up in their own pressures and problems and often don't step back and appreciate that something needs to be done. Yet effective treatment is available, usually through your family doctor. He/she may offer treatment themselves or be able to refer you to a mental health specialist or clinic.

**Talking treatments** with a therapist, counsellor or psychologist can be very helpful. Apart from giving you a chance to offload some of your feelings, these will usually involve well-tried and successful approaches like cognitive-behaviour therapy (CBT) or problem-solving therapy. Over several sessions you will be encouraged to identify triggers to your depression and examine how the way you interpret what is happening can affect your mood and emotions. The therapist will work out practical steps and exercises with you to help reverse some of the negative triggers so they no longer have the power to keep you depressed. Everything you say will be confidential – unless your therapist considers that you might be at serious and immediate risk of harming yourself or others.

**Medication** can be very effective in combating depression. Anti-depressants can act as mood lifters and generally have fewer side-effects than other drugs like tranquillisers, etc. It is important to understand that they can take up to three weeks to work – many people give up taking them before they have any positive effect. However, recent research suggests that anti-depressants are not suitable for all young people and, if you are prescribed medication, the doctor should discuss its potential benefits and risks and possible side-effects with you first. You will also need regular reassessment to make sure the drug suits you.

**The best approach for severe depression** will vary from person to person. Often it will involve a combination of treatments, e.g. counselling or talking treatments plus medication and self-help. Simple improvements in diet and exercise can make a vast difference to mood. Anti-depressants can also make you feel better quite quickly but are unlikely to get to the root of what is causing the depression in the first place. Talking therapies such as CBT often have a more permanent result, but you may need to take medication for a while as well. Different people react to different treatments in different ways. You may have to try more than one type of anti-depressant before you and your doctor find one that suits you. You may also find that you don't feel comfortable with your therapist or counsellor. Perhaps you would feel happier talking to a man rather than a woman – or vice versa. Or you may simply not 'click' with them. Just as with drugs, not all therapists are right for all individuals; if you have doubts, don't be scared to ask if you can see someone else instead.

Finding the right combination of approaches can take time – and effort – but your doctor will help with this and you mustn't be afraid to go back and explain what is or isn't working.

## DOC BOX

This is what Adam, a family doctor in a busy south London practice, told us about young people's problems:

*We encourage teenagers to come to talk to us on their own from the age of about fifteen onwards. Often this is difficult as their mum may want to come into the consulting room with them, but we try to be tactful and suggest that the young people may be more comfortable seeing us on their own. I certainly know that someone is often more likely to tell me* about their real worries if their mother isn't breathing down their neck!

Apart from the usual colds and flus, girls tend to come to us with period problems, worries about breast lumps, body image issues — e.g. they're anxious that they're too fat or too thin — acne, contraception and unwanted pregnancy.

Boys often complain about problems of bullying and tend to be worried about acne, their weight and size and whether they are developing fast enough at puberty. Lots of boys are also worried about the possibility of sexually transmitted infections.

Of course, these are all physical problems, but a number of them have associated mental health issues, and we have many young people showing stress-related symptoms like depression, panic attacks or mood disturbance. These are often related to events in their life, such as a break-up with a boyfriend or girlfriend, abuse in the family or even the fear of being made homeless. We also see many young people with eating disorders.

We are very fortunate in our practice to have three mental health nurse counsellors, one male and two female. This means that young people with mental or emotional problems can usually be assessed quite quickly and given ongoing help and support where necessary. If we are really worried about someone or think they might be at risk of damaging themselves, we can usually get them an appointment to see the mental health team at the local hospital straight away, even if it means taking them to the A and E department and waiting with them.

My advice to any young person worrying about mental or physical health is to get advice as soon as possible. I know that the thought of talking to your family doctor might be frightening or embarrassing, but he or she will be sympathetic. You might find it a lot easier to bring an advocate — e.g. a friend or family member — with you for moral support and to help you explain the problem. Or you may want to write your worries down and show them to the doctor. The important thing is that we find out what is troubling you — then we can start doing our job!

### *What if You Didn't Get Treatment for Depression?*

Most people (probably about eighty per cent) would find that their depression eventually went away on its own – but this could take six months or more. That could mean half a year (or longer) of feeling really low and miserable. The remaining twenty per cent would likely get worse, be seriously depressed for two years or more, and may be at risk of serious self-neglect, self-harm or suicide.

Some types of depression can 'flip' from leaving you feeling down and hopeless to overexcited and irrationally determined to do all sorts of things. This is called manic depression or bipolar disorder. The 'up' phase can be even more destructive than the 'down' phase, as a sufferer may lose the power to control their urges. Anything they try or do is taken to the extreme, even if it damages themselves or others.

Whether or not to get treatment is obviously an individual choice, and it is made complicated by the fact that one of the symptoms of depression is lack of motivation. But, unless some-one has been depressed several times before, it is impossible to predict whether they will be one of the sufferers who will get better on their own or who will just get worse. So rather than face many months of feeling wretched and miserable, it would make sense to try out some of the self-help strategies in this chapter and then consider getting help if the depression wasn't lifting.

## Other Common Mental Health Problems

### *Stress and Anxiety Disorders*

It can be good to have some degree of stress in your life. It provides a challenge and helps keep you sharp. But some people are better than others at dealing with stress, and sometimes it all gets too much. An overload of stress can leave you vulnerable to addictions – many people start using alcohol or drugs as a way to combat or escape the stress in their lives. Stress can also lead into depression and, in some people, weaken their immune system so they also become more vulnerable to certain diseases.

Anxiety-related problems are often linked to a particular fear – e.g. of school, exams, abuse – or a specific phobia – e.g. of spiders, injections, crowded or enclosed spaces. These disorders often show up first as physical symptoms (e.g. headaches, upset stomachs or problems with sleeping), but they can also lead to the very unpleasant experience of panic attacks.

**Panic attacks** are your body's reaction to extreme anxiety. Your brain releases powerful chemicals into your bloodstream, getting you ready for a 'fight or flight' response. These chemicals raise your heart rate and your breathing becomes much faster. You may hear the pulse thudding in your head or feel as though your heart is going to jump out of your chest. The sensations can be very frightening, and many people think they are either about to pass out or have a heart attack. Not surprisingly, these unpleasant feelings quickly become linked in your mind with whatever it was that started them off in the first place. You then find yourself even more anxious than before – now you're not only scared of sitting an exam, but also of having a panic attack!

**Phobias** affect your body and brain in the same way. Someone who is scared of spiders may not even be able to pick up a book which they know contains a picture of a spider! Even thinking about it can bring on panic symptoms.

**Obsessions** are often also anxiety related. Sometimes an accident or incident may start them off. It wouldn't be surprising if someone who was knocked down in a traffic accident then became obsessively careful about crossing the road! Obsessions are often linked to fear and become combined in your mind with a series of rituals which you 'have' to do to stop your fears coming true.

**Obsessive-compulsive disorder** is when an obsession leads to a repetitive behaviour that someone feels they have to perform over and over again in order to avert disaster.

## Chloe's Story

Chloe, aged twelve, was often left alone in the house at night when her parents went out. It was an old building with lots of creaking sounds, and she hated lying in bed scared that someone might be trying to break in. She would get up and check that the doors were locked and all the windows were closed several times before she could settle down. Then things got worse, and she found herself getting up to make her security checks time after time after time – even if she knew her parents were in the house. She already knew that everything was locked up, but a feeling inside her said that, unless she carried on checking every door and window, something bad outside would jump in and get her.

## Treatment for Stress and Anxiety Disorders

Although some young people with stress-related disorders may need a short course of medication, most will do very well with talking treatments (therapy). Relaxation training, which concentrates on slowing your breathing and your heart rate, is highly effective with panic attacks and phobias. Counselling in a one-to-one situation or in small groups, or self-help groups via the telephone or Internet, can also be very effective.

## Psychotic Symptoms

These include a wide variety of symptoms that affect the way you perceive and interpret your surroundings and your own thought processes. They may include *hallucinations* – where you see or hear things that aren't really there. One of the commonest types of hallucination is hearing voices. Sometimes these can be friendly, but they can also turn frightening and sound as though they're telling you to do things you know you don't want to do.

Some people suffer from *delusions*. You may be convinced that others are out 'to get you' or that you have powers you have to keep secret from the rest of the world or that your thoughts are being controlled by some other person or being.

Not surprisingly, people with these types of problem quickly feel confused and disorientated. You may have trouble expressing yourself and become withdrawn and moody. Your symptoms may be mistaken for depression at first.

Many, many people experience some of these symptoms at some time in their lives. They can be brought on by severe stress or exhaustion or a high temperature that temporarily affects the way your brain is functioning. For many it's a one-off, isolated (though terrifying) episode, but for others it's a warning of a serious mental illness that needs help – quickly. These illnesses can be dangerous and in some cases can lead to violence against yourself or others. Asking for help or advice can be difficult because you might be scared of people thinking you are 'mad', but often these feelings are due to a simple chemical imbalance in the brain and can be controlled to a large extent with medication and support. Mental health professionals – e.g. counsellors, psychologists, psychiatrists – and family doctors all understand how frightening this type of illness can be and will not be shocked by anything you tell them. It's possible that you may need to go into an adolescent psychiatric unit for a short time while your medication is sorted out, but this also gives you the opportunity to have extra counselling and get lots of advice for coping in the future. Many people are also treated as out-patients, but it's important to return for regular check-ups and – very important – not to stop taking your medication suddenly without your doctor's advice.

## Jonathan's Story

Jonathan was eighteen and in his first year at college when he started acting strangely. He was convinced that there was a plot to kill him and that people were talking about him behind his back. He mentioned it to several of his friends over several days, and two of them were increasingly worried about him. He told them he was hearing voices, which said they were trying to protect him, but he was scared that he was still in danger. This seemed to get worse over a period of about three days, and on the Sunday morning Jonathan's friends talked about it together and then told him they were so concerned that they wanted him to see someone at the Student Medical Centre the next day. Jonathan agreed and even seemed a bit better for a while. However, the friends were still very worried, so they made sure they stayed with him all day and sat up late at night with him, talking and listening to music. He assured them he was fine and feeling better and would definitely go to see a doctor in the morning, so they left him in his room to go to sleep at about one a.m.

Jonathan didn't appear at breakfast the next day, and when they went to his room he wasn't there either. It seems that he had gone to bed for at least part of the night, but at around six a.m. on the Monday morning had walked down the road to a bridge over a railway line and thrown himself off in front of an oncoming train.

Jonathan's friends were shocked and upset, and at first they blamed themselves for what had happened. The police came to ask questions and they realised that other people had been worried about Jonathan too, but nobody had been able to stop him from killing himself. It seems likely that Jonathan had suffered from an acute psychotic episode. This is a type of mental illness that causes you to hear, see and believe things that aren't true and don't exist. Jonathan may have thought that he was going to be killed and that taking his own life was the only way he could see to escape the danger and the pain.

For more information and advice about mental health problems, look in the Contacts section. Young Minds is a particularly good source of information both for parents and carers as well as young people suffering from any kind of mental health problem.

# 4 Compulsive and Damaging Behaviours, Part 1:
## Self-Harm and Eating Disorders

**This chapter covers:**

- What Are Compulsive Behaviours?
- Self-Harming Behaviours
- Why Do People Self-Harm?
- Treatments for Self-Harm
- Eating Disorders
- Anorexia Nervosa
- Dangers of Anorexia
- Treatment for Anorexia
- Bulimia Nervosa
- Dangers of Bulimia
- Treatment for Bulimia
- What to Do if You Think a Friend Has an Eating Disorder

## What Are Compulsive Behaviours?

These are behaviours that start out either as an experiment or matter of choice but eventually become compulsive, i.e. beyond your control. Some of these, such as gambling and excessive exercise, are relatively socially acceptable, but over time you may find that they disrupt your everyday life and cause problems.

*I've always been interested in fitness and exercise, but I think my problem started when I was about fourteen and my dad commented* that I was getting 'a bit of a tummy'. I tried cutting down on food but I hated feeling hungry so I started doing sit-ups and exercises instead. This worked really well, and I loved the feeling of being able to keep my body in shape. I started going running before school and in the evening and doing about an hour of sit-ups, etc. before I went to sleep. It was great, because it meant I could eat whatever I wanted and often I really pigged out. People couldn't believe how much I could eat, and they all envied me being 'naturally slim', but they never knew how much effort I put into working off the calories! But then it started to take over and all I could think of was food and exercise. There wasn't any time for friends or anything else. It wasn't until I was nineteen that I began to realise there was something seriously wrong.

*Sara, 21*

I started buying scratch cards mainly because it was easy and nobody ever asked my age. At first it was only one or two, but, after I won £50, I started spending any cash I could get hold of – even some that wasn't mine! I know I can't afford it, but it's like a bug has got hold of me and, each time I think I might win, everything else seems worth it.

*Jake, 17*

Other compulsive behaviours are less socially accepted, more secretive and more obviously dangerous to your health. The most common are self-harming behaviours and eating disorders, e.g. anorexia nervosa and bulimia nervosa.

These behaviours often start 'innocently' in response to another problem in a young person's life. They are often an attempt by the person to make themselves feel more in control of something unpleasant or painful that is happening in their lives. For a while this strategy may seem to work, but the behaviour quickly becomes compulsive, i.e. totally out of control and increasingly damaging to the sufferer. However, because it's being done in secret and because the behaviour itself revolves around secrecy, it can be a long time, even many years, before the sufferer decides they need help – or the situation is discovered and help is made available.

## Self-Harming Behaviours

When someone deliberately hurts themselves, this is called self-injury or self-harm. People do a variety of things, but they are NOT usually trying to kill themselves. Instead, it is more often an attempt to make themselves feel better or to cope with a difficult problem.

Behaviours include:

- cutting or burning the skin;
- constantly picking at scabs from old injuries;
- pulling out hair;
- hitting arms/legs with a hard object;
- starving or binge-eating and vomiting;
- taking overdoses of over-the-counter painkillers, e.g. aspirin or paracetamol.

Some people feel that many young people who binge-drink, take drugs or smoke too much are also behaving in a deliberately self-harmful way. The young people in question may argue that their use of these substances is purely recreational but in many cases addiction plays a part. For more about addictive behaviours and addictions, see Chapter 5.

### *Facts about Self-Harm*
- About one in thirteen young people self-harm every year – and the number is increasing.
- About one in eight of self-harmers will end up in hospital.

- Over their whole lives, about one in six people has at least one episode of self-harming behaviour.
- Self-harm is four times more common in girls than in boys.
- A small number of people do it because their friends are doing it or they've read about it or seen it on TV.

### Why do People Self-Harm?

Most people who self-harm are not trying to commit suicide – they use self-harm as a way of coping with or controlling their emotions and feelings.

Someone who self-injures is usually emotionally distressed. They may have been abused – physically, emotionally or sexually – or have a poor level of self-esteem. They often describe themselves as 'useless' or 'worthless'. Many sufferers say they see self-harm as something they are able to have control over, even if they feel out of control in the rest of their lives.

It's much more common in girls than in boys, and self-harmers usually inflict their injuries in secret, so they've often been doing it for a long time before anyone notices. People who cut their arms try to disguise this by wearing long-sleeved tops, so someone who insists on keeping covered up, even on a really hot day, could be hiding scars or burns on their arms and legs.

The injuries can result in long-term scarring and, because the knives or razor blades that people cut with are often not sterile, many people can get infections. Sufferers are usually aware of the dangers of self-harm but still find it very difficult to stop.

## Mel's Story

When my dad left, my mum went to pieces and I knew it was important that I stayed strong for her. She often said she didn't know what she'd do without me, but that didn't stop her from drinking so much that she was asleep by the end of EastEnders most nights. I used to really worry about what would happen to us and angry with her, but knew I couldn't say anything. It felt like it was all going round and round inside me until I would explode. One night I was doing my homework, listening to her snoring in her chair when I picked up a pair of scissors and started poking the tips into my arm just above the elbow. It was like I was watching myself, waiting to see what happened. I felt the pain and there was even a bit of blood, but it made me feel better about everything else. It blocked out all my worries about my mum.

Afterwards, I bathed my arm in cold water and didn't think anything of it for a few days until things got bad again. After that, I did it two or three times a week. I bought some antiseptic cream and always made sure that the cuts and scratches were clean, and by wearing shirts at school and long-sleeved tops for the rest of the time no one ever knew. When it was summer I said I didn't want to sunbathe because I was scared of skin cancer and always made an excuse not to go swimming. On the odd occasions when someone did notice, I just said I'd scratched myself on brambles. It became part of my life, and I relied on it to keep me sane. But at the same time I knew it wasn't right, and I often thought about trying to get some help. But who could I have asked? I didn't think that anyone else would understand, and I certainly didn't want anyone to know what things were like at home.

Then, when I was seventeen, the scratches got infected. I must have been careless, but I got really ill with a blood infection. I put more cream on and tried to go to school as normal but ended up in the medical room. I was holding my arm because it hurt so much, and the teacher on duty asked what was the matter with me. I didn't know what to say, and she rolled up my sleeve to have a look. I thought she'd be horrified, but she just said I needed to see a doctor and called my mum to say I needed to go to the hospital casualty department. They gave me some pills for the infection, but they also said I needed to see a counsellor. I didn't want to do it but, because both the teacher and my mum knew by then, I realised I'd have to.

It took nearly a year of counselling and therapy for me to give up self-harming. I knew I wanted to put it behind me, but after so long it was really difficult. I couldn't believe how well the counsellor and some of the teachers at school understood what I was going through. They were really supportive, and with their help I got all sorts of things sorted out. My mum is even trying to tackle her drinking now, so life is much better at home as well.

*Mel, 19*

### Treatments for Self-Harm

It seems likely that quite a few people who self-harm may do it for only a short time. Either they are 'trying it out' because they have seen or heard of other young people self-harming – or the problem that triggered it goes away. However, anyone who continues to self-harm should be encouraged to get help. Their doctor may be able to refer them to a specialist who will try to help them look at the reasons why they are behaving in this way. Therapists accept that it is a difficult behaviour to change and that the young person isn't going to be able to stop easily. For any treatment or therapy to work, the self-harmer must want to change. Psychologists and counsellors usually use a form of therapy called cognitive behaviour therapy (CBT). This helps people to look at the feelings that are triggering the self-harm and try to find other ways of dealing with them.

As well as CBT, therapists often use a variety of other treatments or approaches. The idea is always to find some other, safer way of expressing and dealing with emotions when things get bad.

**Finding someone to talk to** can make a big difference. Sufferers say they need to be listened to rather than 'talked at', as this doesn't help them at all! Talking can be face to face, but for some people it's easier to talk to a stranger, e.g. Samaritans (see Contacts).

**Relaxation techniques**, such as making a relaxation tape and practising how to use it, can be helpful when the urge to self-harm becomes difficult to resist.

**Expressing feelings in different ways** can help a young person to let go of the difficult feelings behind the self-harm, e.g. writing them down, painting or doing something really physical like screaming or tearing things up or beating up pillows or cushions.

**Physical exercise** is also a useful distraction and a way of releasing tension and aggression. But this needs to be done cautiously – you don't want to turn self-harm into exercise addiction.

**Distraction activities** like TV or music or making positive plans not to be on your own can also help.

Therapists know very well that giving advice to young people doesn't always go down well. They will try to give examples of what other people have found useful. It's important that the self-harmer feels in control of their own therapy and eventual cure. No one can force it on them. As with any therapy, anything said will be kept confidential, unless the therapist thinks you may be at risk of suicide or of harming others.

# Eating Disorders

Most people have heard of anorexia and bulimia, but there is a wide range of other eating disorders as well. One example is *selective eating*, where a person refuses to eat anything apart from a small number of particular foods. This leads to an imbalanced diet, which may be lacking in essential nutrients. Another example is *restrictive eating*, where someone becomes obsessive about the number of calories they eat. They may not lose much weight but, as with all eating disorders, obsession with food – whether it's the fear of it, craving for it or control over it – takes over their life.

Sometimes, perhaps because of an experience of choking when food went down the wrong way or of being sick after eating a particular food, a person can develop a fear that food will choke them. They may just avoid a particular type or texture of food or they could find it very difficult to eat anything at all except for liquids or very soft food. Like many eating disorders this often starts gradually but then grows to such an anxiety that it becomes impossible for them to eat in front of other people or anywhere outside their own home.

## Rebecca's Story

Rebecca's problems started when she was thirteen and caught a really bad stomach bug that made her throw up over and over again. She had always hated being sick, and this time she was throwing up so often there was nothing left to come out and all the dry heaving really hurt her chest and throat. When she started getting better, Rebecca found that eating something like dry toast or a biscuit made her throat feel scratchy or uncomfortable, and she started to worry that this would make her be sick again. She tried to stick to soft foods like soup, scrambled eggs, yoghurt and cold drinks, thinking that the problem would clear up, but every time she was faced with a plate of normal food that she had to chew before swallowing she began to feel panicky and worried she'd be sick again.

It wasn't quite so bad at home, because she could choose what she wanted to eat and go to the bathroom and spit things out if they made her feel peculiar. But at school she stopped having proper lunches and just had a yoghurt and a banana instead. When friends invited her round, she always said she had to go home when it was time to have something to eat, because she didn't know how to explain that she could no longer eat normal food. She refused to go on a school trip to France for the same reason, and it wasn't until the whole family went on holiday and were eating meals together in the hotel that Rebecca's mother realised there was a real problem. The first few days were awful, because she kept nagging Rebecca to eat and treated her like a baby, but on the fourth day Rebecca broke down and told her mum how she felt.

When they got home, Rebecca's mum rang up a helpline for parents and, without giving her name, described the problem. She was very surprised to learn that vomit phobia was quite common and that most GPs would either be able to offer support or refer a sufferer for some counselling. She discussed this with Rebecca, who agreed to go with her mum to talk to their GP. He made an appointment with a counsellor for Rebecca, and together they worked out a staged programme of steps for Rebecca to work towards. The counsellor also taught her some relaxation exercises, and together they made a tape for Rebecca to play when she felt panicky and sick. After three sessions, there was a real improvement, and at the end of six Rebecca felt brave enough to stay over at her friend's house and have supper with her family.

## Anorexia Nervosa

### Facts About Anorexia Nervosa
- Anorexia affects as many as one in a hundred girls.
- Boys can get anorexia – but only about one in two thousand.
- As many as one in five sufferers of severe anorexia will die from it.

Anorexia nervosa often starts at around the age of thirteen or fourteen and, if you're a teenage girl, you probably already know, or know of, someone who has it. You may also even have secretly wished that you could 'catch' it yourself in order to lose some weight. But anorexia is a serious illness that can kill or cause serious health problems, such as infertility, osteoporosis and seizures. Different researchers and doctors have reported different rates of death, but about a fifth of all people who have anorexia badly enough to be admitted to hospital may eventually die from it.

Sufferers can have problems in trying to eat normally for the rest of their lives.

Someone with anorexia may:

- lose weight, even when they are already at the lower end of normal weight for their age and height;
- have an obsessive fear of fatness. Typical anorexics worry desperately that they are fat and are extremely anxious that they shouldn't gain any weight or become fat in the future;
- have a distorted belief about their weight and/or size. Although anyone looking at them can see that they are very thin, when they look at themselves in a mirror they believe that they see a fat person looking back;
- stop having periods;
- cover up with jumpers and baggy clothes – partly to disguise their shape and size, but also because their body doesn't have enough fuel to keep them warm;
- make excuses to skip meals, but still be fascinated by food and cooking;
- be particularly obsessed about food – arrange it carefully on their plate, eat it in a certain order, etc.;
- exercise obsessively – often secretly at night;

Most people who develop anorexia are not usually very overweight to begin with. There are many different theories about why some of the thousands of people who start a diet to lose a few pounds then go on to develop anorexia. Some people have large or over-weight family members and are terrified of ending up like them. Others see dieting as a way of being in control of one part of their lives when everything else may seem chaotic or painful. Being able to control their eating and their weight increases their self-esteem, making them feel less vulnerable. Other young people say they diet obsessively so that people won't notice them or because they don't want the body changes, such as the develop-ment of breasts, associated with growing up.

Popular media must also take some share of the blame. TV, magazines and advertising all promote the idea that people should be slim and beautiful. Many fashion models are severely under-weight, and the clothes they parade on the catwalk and through the pages of fashion magazines would often look completely different on anyone of 'normal' shape and size. Even teenage magazines that offer 'real-life' stories and features are often guilty of choosing unrealistically tiny models for their illustrations rather than ones the size and shape of their average reader.

In girls, certain groups seem to be more at risk of developing anorexia. These include:

- girls from wealthy or privileged backgrounds;
- those who are perfectionists or are very eager to please;
- those who have very set or 'black-and-white' ways of thinking;
- girls whose sisters or mothers had anorexia or other eating disorders;
- girls who are depressed or under a lot of stress.

# Susie's Story

Until I was about twelve I was a really happy person, good at schoolwork and usually top of the class. I was really pleased with my Year 6 SATs tests, and my mum and dad paid for me to go on a pony-trekking holiday as a reward for doing so well. I wasn't quite as happy in Year 7, as most of my old friends didn't move to the same secondary school as me, so I felt a bit out of my depth. All the other girls seemed much older than me, and they thought anyone who was interested in horses was a bit sad! I still worked really hard, as I'd begun to think that I'd like to be a vet when I left school, and Mum had told me that for this I would need at least three A-grades at A-level.

Even though my new friends at school teased me about riding, I still loved it and managed to fit in a lesson each Saturday morning. The only problem was that as I was growing really fast and getting much heavier I was worried that I'd be made to change to another pony at the stables. One day a new stable lad arrived. He was about sixteen and also interested in going to veterinary college. He was really friendly, and I soon started looking forward even more to my Saturday riding lessons. Then I overheard him talking to another stable hand about that `plump posh girl' and saying he felt sorry for her poor horse. I felt sick with shame and disgust when I suddenly realised that he was laughing about me. I cried all the way home in the car, but wouldn't tell Mum what the problem was. I realised there was only one solution – to lose weight and then go back to the stables and show him how pretty I could be.

I had never really thought much about it before, but when I told one of the girls at school it turned out that about half the girls in our class were on diets. Everyone gave me loads of information about calories and exercise and some girls even told me that they made themselves sick straight after meals so that they would lose weight quickly.

At first, I just cut out snacks and puddings and I lost one or two pounds each week. Then I got a bit impatient and began missing out lunch at school. Even though I was starving hungry, I liked the feeling of power that I got from refusing to eat. After that I became even stricter with myself and would tell Mum that I was eating big lunches at school, so only wanted an apple for breakfast. Then I would have no lunch, come home and lie about it, saying I was really full up because it was stew and dumplings, etc., so I would eat only a piece of fruit for supper too. I cut out all drinks except water. In the end I was surviving on a couple of apples and about eight glasses of water a day, plus an occasional piece of chewing gum.

The main thing I can remember about this time is that I was constantly hungry. My stomach ached all the time, and I was always freezing cold. Even though it was May, I wandered around the house in a couple of sweaters and insisted that the central heating was on. But I was pleased with how thin I was getting. My mum's friends kept stopping her in the street and asking her if I was all right. I did try to make myself throw up, but never really got the hang of it.

Of course, Mum got suspicious, but I just got cross and angry with her whenever she tried to raise the subject. I stopped having periods, and I knew this would bother her, so I kept on asking her to get me sanitary towels so she didn't realise what was going on. Whenever my parents went out, I used to run up and down the stairs about twenty times to burn up more calories and also to see if I could improve on my 'personal best' time for each circuit.

This all went on for about six months until we broke up for the summer holiday. Then it got more difficult, because Mum was on my case! She started to talk to me nearly every day about my weight, asking me what was bothering me and so on. In the end I gave in and agreed to talk to my doctor.

Luckily, Mum let me go in and see the doctor on my own – I would have felt really embarrassed talking in front of her. The doctor was very kind and gentle, and somehow I found myself telling her all about the diet and confessing that now I just couldn't stop. I felt almost addicted to the idea of getting as thin as possible. The doctor weighed and measured me and showed me how thin I was for my height. I couldn't believe it – I had lost over four stones in only a few months. She explained about some of the problems that anorexia can cause. I felt very confused, because although I could see on the chart I looked too thin I still felt quite fat and I wasn't at all keen on the idea of putting some weight back on. I thought that if I started eating `properly' again I just wouldn't be able to stop.

Since then, I've been going to see a counsellor who is a specialist in helping people with eating disorders. It has taken almost two years for me to gradually gain one stone, and I feel comfortable at this weight. My periods started again last month – a mixed blessing! I still feel anxious every time I have to sit down for a meal, and it is hard not to get up and go running up and down the stairs to compensate. My counsellor says I may find the whole subject of food and eating really difficult to deal with for a long time yet.

Now I've read lots about anorexia I realise many people ignore the problems for even longer than I did. Some go to hospital for treatment in the end. I feel I was probably lucky to have such a nagging mum.

As for the gorgeous boy – well, I'll probably never know what would have happened. I went back to riding a few months ago when I was starting to feel a bit better, but he was no longer working there. The owner said he had moved to another placement because of an `attitude problem'. Still, by now I'm well and truly over him.

*Susie, 16*

## Dangers of Anorexia

Apart from a very real risk of death from starvation, anorexia can also cause long-term damage to the sufferer's body:

**Dehydration and damage to vital organs** – because of vomiting or using excessive over-the-counter medicines to hurry food through the digestive system. This means that water and salts are lost along with the loose stools, causing severe chemical imbalances. This can interfere with the electrical activity of your heart, even causing heart failure. Dehydration can also cause kidney failure and kidney stones.

**Sore throat or mouth and bad teeth** – caused when people make themselves sick. Vomit contains a lot of acid from the stomach and this can damage the oesophagus – the tube that takes food from the mouth to the stomach, or the back of the teeth. In some cases vomit spills over into the windpipe and lungs and can cause pneumonia (a lung infection). And, if you are making yourself vomit a lot, you could get a tear in the oesophagus, which could bleed so you start to vomit up blood.

**Anaemia, vitamin and mineral deficiency** – You may become anaemic if the amount of iron in the diet is too low. This can make you very tired. A diet that is very low in fats and vitamins can also lead to dry, flaky and irritated skin.

**Bone damage** – Sufferers can lose calcium from their bones, so later in life they may get brittle bones (osteoporosis) and have lots of painful fractures.

**Stunted growth** – In younger patients (under eighteen), growth can slow down or stop altogether. Although you may grow a little more if you get better, anorexia often stops you growing to the height you 'should' have been.

**Brain damage** – In very severe cases your brain matter may start to shrink, leading to fits or seizures.

**Infertility** – Being severely underweight stops ovulation, because your body is not getting enough nourishment to support a pregnancy. Long-term sufferers of anorexia can find it very hard to get pregnant – although when your weight returns to normal this problem usually corrects itself.

### Treatment for Anorexia

Sometimes sufferers are admitted to hospital because it is too dangerous for them to stay at home. They need expert treatment, and the aim of this, whether at home or in hospital, is to help them gain enough weight so that their body can start to recover from starvation and function again properly. In girls, a good clue that a sufferer is recovering is that her periods start again.

Even if they don't go into hospital, most anorexics will need support from mental health experts to help them change the way they think about their body size and shape, and their relationship to food. In many cases, it is useful for the whole family to attend sessions with the doctor or counsellor, as there are often wider problems that need to be talked through. In some cases, girls are also treated with medication, which may help them to feel better about themselves and what's going on in their lives.

# Bulimia Nervosa

### Facts About Bulimia Nervosa

- Approximately three to five per cent of young women suffer from bulimia – it exists in men but is much less common.
- Bulimia tends to start later than anorexia – most commonly in the late teens or early adulthood.
- Because it's a 'hidden' disease, sometimes with no obvious

symptoms or dramatic weight loss, it often goes unnoticed by family or friends.

The main symptom of bulimia is episodes of binge-eating where the sufferer stuffs themselves with large amounts of food, often high in carbohydrates – like bread, biscuits, cake and ice cream. Then, because they feel guilty and are scared of putting on weight they feel they have to 'get rid' of it somehow. Often, this means making themselves sick. However, some bulimics use over-the-counter laxatives to speed up the passage of food through their digestive system instead of vomiting, or spend hours exercising obsessively in an effort to work off the excess calories.

The sufferer may have a single episode of bulimia and then nothing more for a while, but eventually the binge-eating episodes get closer and closer together and life becomes increasingly chaotic. A bulimic will start planning times when they can be alone to eat and eat until they are literally sick. They become completely obsessed with food and may even start borrowing, selling off possessions and stealing in order to fund their 'habit'.

### An Emotional Reaction

Bulimia often starts in the mid- to late-teenage years when something happens to make the sufferer feel bad about themselves. It could be a break-up with a boyfriend, name-calling or bullying by other people at school, or the failure to win a much-wanted part in a school play. The highly obsessive binging and purging (i.e. getting rid of the food eaten) behaviour of bulimia is an attempt to make the sufferer feel better about themselves. Further attacks or episodes after a longer period of normal eating are usually set off by stress, depression or other emotional problems.

## Dangers of Bulimia

There are probably many bulimics who never seek help or treatment and either get better on their own after a few months or have recurring periods of bulimia throughout their lives. Some young women ask for treatment only when they want to have a baby and are scared that their irregular eating habits will either make getting pregnant difficult or damage the baby in the womb.

A sufferer is far less likely to die from bulimia than from anorexia, but sometimes the two can merge and a bulimic may develop full-blown anorexia. Also, just as in anorexia, the repeated vomiting or use of laxatives can cause dehydration and chemical imbalances, leading to organ damage. Acids from your stomach (which were never designed to come into contact with your oesophagus) can eat away at your oesophageal lining and throat, causing ulcers as well as staining and destroying the back of your teeth. However, the main risk of bulimia is the fact that it leads to a feeling of being alone and trapped into a cycle of behaviour that you think no one else could possibly understand. This isolation can lead to depression and even attempted suicide.

## Treatment for Bulimia

Many sufferers never receive treatment, although their bulimia can stay with them throughout their lives. However, there is treatment available, even though, as with any type of self-harm, you have to make a positive decision that you want to overcome the problem. Your family doctor (GP) will understand the difficulties and should be able to start treatment or refer you to a specialist centre for an out-patient clinic appointment. In the UK, the Eating Disorders Association (see Contacts) can also give excellent and unbiased advice about treatments available.

Some of the best results involve cognitive-behaviour therapy (CBT). This is a talking therapy based on examining how your feelings about yourself make you think you have to behave in a certain way. This type of therapy, either one to one with a counsellor or in small groups, can help you look at some of the emotional triggers for your episodes of binging. It helps overcome any basic unhappiness and lack of self-confidence, so that a temptation to binge again becomes less attractive or powerful.

Some people also benefit from a short course of antidepressants, but these should only ever be taken under the guidance of and with regular check-ups from a doctor.

## What to Do if You Think a Friend Has an Eating Disorder

Because people with anorexia or bulimia are so secretive and can go to great lengths to hide their altered eating habits, it is often best friends who are the first to suspect that something is wrong. If you have a friend who you think may be suffering from an eating disorder, then you should try to talk to them about it first. Don't be angry with them – just say you are worried and would like to understand what it is that's happening to them.

Encourage them to get help, perhaps by talking first of all to a young people's or specialist eating disorders helpline (see Contacts for suggestions). This allows them to keep some control, because they don't have to give their name or address and they can stop the call at any time. They may be unwilling to get help, and this can leave you feeling frustrated and anxious. It won't help if you shout or try to make them feel guilty about what they're doing, because they're likely to feel pretty low anyway.

However, if you have serious worries, then it's important that you don't keep them to yourself. Both anorexia and bulimia can seriously damage the sufferer's health, and anorexia can – and does – kill. If your friend really isn't willing to get help, you need to share your concerns with your parents or another adult (e.g. a teacher) as soon as possible. You could also ring a helpline (see Contacts) to ask for advice on raising the subject with your friend and the best ways to help their particular situation. Your friend may be angry, but you can explain that you're doing it because you care about them and aren't prepared to see them put themselves in danger like this.

# 5 Compulsive and Damaging Behaviours, Part 2:
## Addictions - Legal and Illegal

**This chapter covers:**
- What Is Addiction?
- Habit-Forming Behaviour
- Why Do People Become Addicted?
- How Would You Recognise That You Have a Problem?
- Where Would You Go to Get Help?
- Legally and Socially Accepted Drugs
- Illegal Drugs
- The Most Commonly Used Illegal Drugs

When people talk about addiction, they often focus on the things you might get addicted to, such as alcohol, cigarettes and drugs. While this view of the problem is important – and each of these things has its own particular dangers – it's also useful to think about what being addicted – to anything – actually means.

## What Is Addiction?

Addiction is a craving for and/or dependency on something that is psychologically or physically habit-forming.

When you think of an addict (someone who is addicted), the usual images that come to mind are drug addicts desperate to raise the money for their next hit or sad old alcoholics sitting on park benches clutching their half-empty cans of cider. But these are extreme examples, and many more people suffer from addictions than you might imagine.

Some people are addicted to non-prescription drugs, e.g. simple painkillers that you can buy over the counter in a pharmacy or even from supermarkets. They may have started taking them when they were getting headaches during revision for an exam or to help with bad period pains. The initial problem has probably disappeared, but they now feel anxious and shaky when they don't have the pills in their pocket ready to take 'just in case'. Others can become dependent on caffeine – found in coffee and cola drinks – and they often get severe headaches if they suddenly stop or cut down their intake.

Many people are addicted to types of behaviour. Sometimes called psychological addiction, this can involve things that do you little harm, such as switching your light on and off ten times before you go to sleep, not stepping on cracks in the pavement or exercising excessively. More extreme examples can become damaging and destructive, e.g. eating disorders and self-harm.

### *Habit-Forming Behaviour*

A habit is something that you have become used to doing to the extent that you don't really think about it consciously – you just do it. Some habits are obviously useful to develop – most people are in the habit of brushing their teeth twice each day, for instance. But some habits may be difficult to break. These include things like biting your nails or, for some people, having chocolate after every meal or having a cigarette when they have some alcohol. You are often encouraged to try to develop 'good' habits – such as exercising regularly or ringing your family regularly if you're away from home.

You have to do something about thirty times before it becomes a habit. So, for example, you may decide you are going to start running three times a week. Keeping it up for ten weeks, i.e. thirty runs, is enough for most people to have got used to this new activity and then to be able to keep doing it without giving it much thought. The same thing applies to something like dieting – after thirty days on a calorie-controlled diet, you would probably have become used to a new way of eating and wouldn't have to think about it so much. The changes then become automatic – part of a new habit.

For many people, such habits can develop into addictions. Whether this happens depends on the nature of the person's behaviour and the properties of the drug or substance they are taking. Many legal substances (including cigarettes and alcohol) and illegal drugs (such as crack and heroin) cause a physical addiction as the body starts to need them to feel normal. Most addictions start as a way for someone to escape the pressures or boredom of their life. This is generally true whether it's someone taking drugs on a Friday night or going way over their credit card limit buying clothes they might never wear.

BAD HABITS

## Why Do People Become Addicted?

We don't really know why some people get addicted and others don't. We do know that even if an addict manages to break one particular addiction, they'll still be vulnerable to forming other addictions – particularly when they're under stress or pressure. Such people are described as having an addictive personality.

We know that in some families there seems to be a pattern of addiction – perhaps one parent being an alcoholic and their son or daughter having a drug addiction. So there may be a genetic (inherited) tendency to develop addictions. Another explanation could be that in families like these, addictive behaviour just seems normal. If someone grows up with their parents taking illegal drugs, they have easy access to supplies and may think it is the usual thing to do. On the other hand, some children of addicts – e.g. children of very heavy smokers – become even more determined not to become addicted themselves.

## How Would You Recognise That You Have a Problem?

- If you are starting to plan your daily life around a behaviour or substance and changing your plans to make sure that you can do the activity or get enough of the substance.
- If you start to need more and more of the same substance to feel 'good'.
- If you develop symptoms like shaking, sweating or vomiting when you try to stop taking the substance.
- If you start to see or hear strange things when you don't take the substance.

Many addicts say – and honestly believe – that they can give up any time they want. If you are addicted, you'll find your mind and/or body becomes fixed on whatever it is you're trying to avoid – and this means you need help!

## *Where Would You Go to Get Help?*

You only have to look on the Internet to see that there are different support groups for every possible kind of addiction. Some of them are listed in the Contacts section at the back of this book. However, you might find it useful to talk to someone closer to home first. It's often said that admitting you have a problem is the first step to overcoming addiction, and it certainly makes it easier if you have a friend or family member supporting you and fighting your corner.

You might want to start by talking to your GP – they will be able to help you determine whether you have a problem or not and suggest ways in which to get help. Even if you decide that you are not ready to tackle the problem when you first go to talk about it, your GP can still give you facts and advice about possible future problems. And they can tell you how to get in contact with support services when you do decide that you want some help.

We know that in order for someone to be successfully treated for an addiction, they have to want that treatment themselves – it's no good if they go along just because a parent or partner is worried about them.

Treatments for problems like drug addiction range from controlled use of the substance, when a doctor or clinic will agree to supply you with a set amount per day, through to supporting you as you attempt to stop taking the substance completely. Some clinics choose a different approach depending on the specific needs of the client. Addicts also need a lot of support to get their whole life back in order, and this may include help to get out of the situation and surroundings in which they developed their addiction.

# Legal and Socially Accepted Drugs

## *Alcohol*

We have already mentioned alcohol in Chapter 2 in relation to the huge impact it has in terms of affecting people's behaviour and contributing to accidents and risk-taking.

This section looks at how many young people drink alcohol, how much they are drinking and the short-term and long-term effects of drinking too much.

**Note:** In the UK it is illegal for someone under eighteen to buy alcohol in a shop or a pub, but there is no specific age at which you are allowed to drink alcohol in the home.

### SOME FACTS AND FIGURES ABOUT ALCOHOL AND YOUNG PEOPLE

The government collects facts and figures about alcohol use in different age groups. Other studies are carried out in schools – where pupils are asked to complete questionnaires stating how much alcohol they drank in the last week and whether they have ever been drunk. Results from the surveys show that:

- one in twenty eleven-year-olds drinks alcohol most weeks;
- half of all fifteen-year-olds drink alcohol most weeks;
- in the ten years between 1990 and 2000, the amount of alcohol that young people drank doubled;
- people in the UK drink more alcohol than people in most other European countries;
- many young people now binge-drink. This means that they drink a large amount of alcohol so that they become really drunk several times each week;
- three-quarters of fifteen-year-olds have got drunk at least once, and more than a quarter have got drunk more than twenty times;

- a thousand young people under fifteen are admitted to hospital each year with alcohol poisoning;
- by the age of fifteen, the average amount of alcohol drunk each week by girls who are drinking is fourteen units – the top of the government's suggested limit;
- for boys aged fifteen, the average is about twenty-four units – three more than the top of the government's suggested limits.

## SO HOW MUCH CAN YOU SAFELY DRINK?

The maximum amount of alcohol per week that you should not exceed if you want to avoid health problems is: twenty-one units for males and fourteen for females.

## WHAT IS A UNIT?

A unit is a specific amount of alcohol. Because some drinks are much stronger than others – spirits are stronger than lager or wine, for instance – the same volume of one drink can contain more units than another. As a guideline, the amount of popular drinks containing one unit of alcohol is:

- half a pint of ordinary beer or lager (between five and seven per cent) – not especially strong beers like Export or Special Brew, which can contain more than twice the amount of alcohol;
- one small glass of wine (the sort of glass you are served in a pub – at home people often use bigger glasses);
- about two-thirds of a bottle of alcopops.

## WHY DO PEOPLE DRINK?

This may seem like a stupid question – you may think everyone drinks to get drunk as quickly as possible! There are other reasons, though. Young people in research groups say that they drink in order to:

- show to themselves and others that they are mature – drinking is seen as an adult activity;
- have fun;
- feel relaxed and confident;
- test their own limits;
- enjoy the taste.

'WELL – IT'S ONLY ONE GLASS!'

**HOW MUCH ALCOHOL DOES IT TAKE TO MAKE SOMEONE DRUNK?**
The effect that alcohol has on a person depends on:

- their size (bigger people and fatter people can tolerate more);
- the rate at which they drink (e.g. four drinks in half an hour will have a greater effect than four drinks in four hours);
- whether they have had a meal before or during the time they are drinking – food slows down the absorption of alcohol;
- the ability of their liver enzymes to break down alcohol;
- their sex.

Most girls start to feel drunk after about three units of alcohol. If they drink more than this for several days every week, it can cause long-term liver damage. Most boys start to feel drunk after about four units. Their bodies are better at breaking down (metabolising) alcohol than girls' bodies are – but boys can get liver damage too.

**Remember:** people who drink at home often drink a lot more alcohol than they realise because they pour double or triple measures.

One of the biggest worries about alcohol is that it can make you take risks and put yourself or others in danger. There is more information on this in Chapter 2.

### WHAT HAPPENS WHEN YOU ARE DRUNK?
Alcohol affects the way your brain functions – it slows down the nerve impulses so you don't think and react as quickly. It is metabolised (broken down) by the liver, which has to work hard to get rid of all the toxins. Toxins cause a headache and make you feel sick. The alcohol also directly irritates the lining of the stomach, and this can make you feel really ill and even cause bleeding. Alcohol in the gut draws out water from the blood-stream, and that means you wee a lot more. So even though you have been drinking fluids, your body can get dehydrated. This also makes you feel really ill – with a headache, dry mouth and generally feeling lousy.

### ALCOHOL POISONING
A thousand under-fifteen-year-olds need emergency treatment for alcoholic poisoning each year. A big problem for teenage drinkers is the fact that alcohol has a bigger effect on their brains

than it does in adults. A young person can quickly become unconscious, which can cause brain damage. They also get cold more quickly, which is especially dangerous if they fall over out in the open, and they have more breathing difficulties than an adult who gets drunk.

Alcohol initially lowers people's inhibitions, so they may feel silly and giggly. But drinking beyond this stage often makes them depressed.

## LONG-TERM DANGERS OF DRINKING TOO MUCH TOO OFTEN

About one in seven young people between the ages of sixteen and twenty-four is dependent on alcohol. Drinking heavily for a long time does seem to put people at risk of dependency and addiction. By drinking heavily we mean drinking so much that you become drunk on several nights each week.

Alcohol is thought to play a part in over 33,000 deaths per year in the UK. In the long term, regular heavy drinking can cause:

- **liver disease** – often fatal, although in some people a liver transplant may save their lives;
- **heart disease and strokes** – because drinking makes blood pressure go up, and this affects the blood vessels of the heart and brain;
- **cancer** – especially of the mouth, throat and oesophagus. Nearly all these cancers can be avoided if people don't smoke and drink;
- **gastritis** – this is irritation of the stomach. It can lead to bleeding, which may be fatal;
- **osteoporosis** – weakening of the bones, leading to fractures;
- **sexual problems** – most people know that too much alcohol can stop you getting an erection, but not everyone realises that long-term alcohol abuse can lead to the testes and penis shrinking!;
- **problems with relationships** – among adults, more than half of those who hit their partners do so while they are drunk;
- **depression** – due to the problems associated with alcohol abuse, such as lack of money and loneliness.

If you are worried that you or a friend may already have a problem with drinking too much alcohol, look at one of the websites or talk to one of the confidential helplines in the Contacts section at the back of this book.

### *Tobacco and Smoking*
Although smoking is legal, health experts agree that nicotine (which is contained in tobacco) is one of the most addictive of all drugs and the hardest to give up. So the best advice here is, if

you haven't started smoking already, don't be tempted to do it!

Tobacco is the dried leaf of a plant. It contains hundreds of chemicals, including the very addictive nicotine, plus other chemicals like tar. These damage the delicate cells inside the lungs, and also harm other parts of the body like blood vessels and the heart.

It is illegal to sell cigarettes to anyone under the age of sixteen.

## SMOKING AND YOUNG PEOPLE

Statistics for 2003 show that:

- more and more people smoke as they get older – one per cent of eleven-year-olds smoke, compared with more than twenty per cent of fifteen-year-olds and about 30 per cent of sixteen-to nineteen-year-olds;
- teenage girls smoke more than boys – although from the age of twenty boys smoke more;
- eleven- to fifteen-year-olds smoked six million cigarettes in 2003;
- some good news: the number of people who have never smoked or just tried it once is increasing slowly.

## SENSATIONS CAUSED BY SMOKING

Some people don't like the effects of nicotine the first time they try a cigarette – it can make them feel sick and a bit dizzy and shaky – while others enjoy it. If they carry on smoking, most people start to enjoy it. Nicotine gets to the brain in a few seconds and makes people feel calm and relaxed. Many girls say that it stops them feeling hungry and this is why they are reluctant to accept that cigarettes can also be harmful.

People who smoke are much more likely to get lung diseases, heart disease and to die early. (There is more information on this in Chapter 8.)

Smoking also affects people around you. If a mother smokes,

her baby is more likely to have breathing problems and deafness. If mothers smoke while they are pregnant, their babies are often smaller than average. The risk of a baby dying from cot death is much higher if their parents smoke.

Smoking makes your clothes, hair and breath smell terrible – and quickly becomes a very expensive habit. It also stains fingers and teeth.

### WAYS TO QUIT

The bad news is that it's *really* hard to stop smoking! Many people have to try several times before they finally quit.

The reason people find it difficult is that they get withdrawal symptoms as the body struggles to manage without nicotine. These include irritability, depression, restlessness and poor concentration. The effects generally last for about four weeks. Many people say that their appetite increases so they eat more and gain weight. This effect can last for several months.

Popular treatments available to help people quit include:

- advice from a doctor or practice nurse or pharmacist;
- behavioural treatments, such as helping people to develop ways to deal with the urge to light up a cigarette when a craving starts;
- nicotine therapy – using patches, gum or inhalers. These can be prescribed by a doctor or you can buy them over the counter;
- drug treatment (with a new type of anti-depressant drug developed to help people stop smoking).

The success rate for most types of treatment is only around ten per cent, so if your first attempt to quit fails, do try another method. You can increase the chance of quitting successfully by doing some practical things, such as:

- set a date to quit – when you know there won't be any other stressful things happening – and getting rid of all your ash-trays, lighters, matches, etc., as well as all your cigarettes;
- give up with a friend so you can support each other;
- if you always smoke in certain places, then avoid those places for a few weeks;
- if you have friends who smoke a lot, try to avoid them for at least six weeks or you might find yourself giving in to a craving;
- visit a dental hygienist to get your teeth cleaned, and brush several times a day so you get used to a cleaner-tasting mouth.

If you do stop, the health benefits kick in very quickly:

- after forty-eight hours there will be no nicotine left in your body, and your sense of taste and smell will improve;
- in about six months coughs and breathing problems usually disappear;
- after five years the risk of a heart attack falls to half that of someone who is still smoking;
- after ten years the chances of having a heart attack falls to the same level as in someone who has never smoked;
- after ten years the risk of getting lung cancer falls to half of that of a smoker.

# Illegal Drugs

Two thousand people die in the UK every year from taking illegal substances. These include drugs, solvents and aerosols.

The manufacture and contents of legally produced substances (like alcohol, cigarettes or painkillers that you buy from a pharmacy) are controlled, so the effect they will have on someone can usually be predicted. It is important to remember that illegally produced substances are *not* controlled and don't come with a label explaining exactly what they contain and the effects they will have.

Substances have different effects on different people in different situations – it is impossible to predict what will happen. Mixing substances complicates things even more. So it is vital to remember that two people can take the same amount of the same drug and one may notice a bigger effect than another – and may have serious side-effects too. There is a huge amount of information on the Internet about drugs – see the section on getting help at the end of the book. One excellent website is *www.talktofrank.com*.

As well as having effects on the person who takes them, drugs can cause problems to those around the taker – their family and friends especially, but also, if the person has to steal to get their supplies, the rest of society. Treatment on the NHS for people who have addictions is very expensive, and at the moment there are not enough treatment programmes to help everyone who is affected.

### *Facts About Drug Use*

Each year the Department of Health collects facts and figures about young people's drug-taking by asking school pupils aged from eleven to fifteen to fill in anonymous questionnaires.

Some facts and figures from the 2003 statistics:

- twenty-one per cent of pupils had taken drugs in the last year;
- twelve per cent had taken drugs in the last month;
- cannabis is easily the most popular drug among this age group
- the number who have tried drugs increases as pupils get older: at age eleven only eight per cent have tried any drugs, compared with thirty-nine per cent at age fifteen;

- among eleven- and twelve-year-olds, more take solvents or volatile substances (aerosols or glue);
- only one per cent of eleven- to fifteen-year-olds had tried heroin, and the same percentage had tried cocaine;
- seventy-five per cent of people who try an illegal drug get it from a friend or relative.

## Drugs and the Law

Many young people are not sure of the facts about what would happen if they were caught taking drugs themselves or supplying them to other people. So here are some reminders. Drugs are divided into three groups called 'classes'. Class-A drugs are thought to do you most harm, and Class-C drugs the least harm. It is illegal to possess (have), give away or deal in any of the three classes of drugs. It is important to know what the consequences could be.

### CLASS-A DRUGS

Includes: heroin, LSD, cocaine, crack, ecstasy. Maximum penalty: seven years in jail for possession, plus an unlimited fine, and up to life in prison and an unlimited fine for dealing.

### CLASS-B DRUGS

Includes: amphetamines (speed). (But Class-B drugs become Class-A drugs if they are prepared for injection.) Maximum penalty: five years in jail for possession, plus an unlimited fine, and up to fourteen years and an unlimited fine for dealing.

### CLASS-C DRUGS

Includes: cannabis, GHB, anabolic steroids and tranquillisers such as Valium and Rohypnol. Maximum penalty: two years in jail for possession, plus an unlimited fine, and up to fourteen years in jail and an unlimited fine for dealing.

### *What Happens if You Are Found With Drugs?*

This depends on the circumstances – such as how old you are, if this is the first time you have been caught and if you only had enough drugs for your own use, or if you were found to have been selling or giving drugs to friends or other people.

If you are under eighteen, you will usually be arrested and taken to a police station to be given a formal warning. Either your parent or a 'responsible adult' – such as a friend's parent if you are staying away from home – will be asked to go to the police station. You may not be charged with an offence if it is the first time and the drugs are class C, and you only had enough for your use. If you are charged and have to go to court, the penalties if you are found guilty can be very serious – see above. Some courts make young offenders complete community-service orders (where they have to do an activity that is good for their local area, such as cleaning graffiti). In most areas, people aged under eighteen are sent to young offenders' institutions rather than prison.

## The Most Commonly Used Illegal Drugs

### *Cannabis*

- Cannabis is a Class-C drug.
- It is also known as dope, grass, marijuana, ganja, pot, hash or weed. A strong form is known as skunk. It comes from a plant that grows all over the world. Sometimes the whole plant is used, or a resin or oil can be extracted.
- It is usually smoked. It is added to tobacco, and the mixture is rolled up to make a type of cigarette called a joint or a spliff. It can also be smoked in a pipe or bong. When people smoke cannabis, they inhale the smoke deeply into their

lungs, holding it there for as long as possible so that it has the strongest effect.

- Cannabis resin is usually hard. The resin is heated gently so that small amounts can be crumbled and added to tobacco.
- Cannabis oil is most commonly added to a cigarette by smearing the cigarette paper with the oil.
- Cannabis can also be eaten with food; it is often used to make biscuits, fudge or cake.

## THE EFFECTS OF CANNABIS

- Cannabis is a depressant drug, so, like alcohol, it can start by relaxing you, but too much can cause depression. It is also hallucinogenic, so it can make you 'high'. An hallucination is when you see or hear something that isn't really there.
- When smoked, cannabis usually takes effect within five to ten minutes.
- When eaten, the effects usually start after thirty to forty-five minutes.
- Common effects are relaxation, then talkativeness and a feeling of being really happy and excited. Sound and colour can seem stronger than usual.
- Cannabis increases the appetite, so many people feel starving hungry after they have taken it.
- Some of the people who take a strong form of cannabis can become paranoid – thinking other people are out to get them or are laughing at them or persecuting them.
- The effects of cannabis usually last for several hours.

## RISKS OF USING CANNABIS

- Regular users may develop a psychological dependence.
- Cannabis can affect coordination, memory and concentration, so it can have a big effect on driving.

- It can cause lung damage, either when smoked on its own or when added to tobacco.
- One type of mental illness – schizophrenia – has been linked to heavy use of cannabis.

## Solvents

- Solvents include lots of things that are found around the house, such as glue, many aerosol cans (such as air fresheners) and gas lighters, as well as paints, paint thinners and correcting fluid.
- It is not illegal to possess them, but if anyone supplies these products to someone under eighteen thinking or knowing they will be used to cause intoxication, then the retailer can be fined or imprisoned.
- It is illegal for retailers to sell gas lighter refills to anyone under eighteen.

### THE EFFECTS OF SOLVENTS

- The effects start quickly – within a few seconds of inhaling the substance.
- Most people feel euphoric to start with – a really intense feeling of happiness and excitement. This feels like being very drunk, and as with being drunk can quickly change into a feeling of sickness, along with blurred vision and drowsiness.
- Some people experience hallucinations.
- The immediate effects last between fifteen and forty-five minutes.

### RISKS OF SOLVENT ABUSE

- In the short term, many people develop spots around the mouth and severe headaches.
- Longer-term effects include damage to the brain and other organs.

- The process of taking the solvents is really dangerous – some people use a plastic bag held over their nose and mouth while they inhale, so as to increase the amount of the substance they get into their lungs. If they then become drowsy, the plastic bag can cause suffocation.
- Sometimes people become unconscious and then vomit – and they can die if they inhale the vomit.
- Many people become psychologically addicted to the effects of solvents, and they can get nasty withdrawal symptoms, including splitting headaches, when they try to stop.

## Cocaine and Crack

- Cocaine and crack are Class-A drugs.
- Possession can result in seven years in prison or a major fine. The penalty for dealing in cocaine can be even higher.
- Other names for cocaine are coke, Charlie and snow.
- Cocaine comes from the leaves of the coca plant. It usually looks like a white powder and most people 'snort' or sniff it through their nose – often using a rolled-up banknote to sniff through.
- Crack is made from cocaine. Crack is sometimes called rocks or base.
- Crack comes in small white crystals. It gets its name from the fact that it is usually heated up and inhaled, and the heating process makes the crystals 'crack'. The effect is very fast and short-acting, and crack is even more addictive than regular cocaine.

### THE EFFECTS OF COCAINE AND CRACK

- It affects the level of a brain transmitter and at first when people sniff it they feel great – really confident and wide awake.
- After a while, most people become dependent on cocaine

and need it just to feel normal. This is often the start of a major addiction to the drug.

## RISKS OF USING COCAINE AND CRACK

- It is highly addictive.
- Psychological dependence on the drug can develop really quickly – if people can't get it they can become very depressed and tired.
- People who take a lot of cocaine or crack can get chest pain and heart problems, and sometimes it causes fits.
- Cocaine can eventually eat away the septum of the nose – the cartilage that separates the two nostrils.
- In some people, it can cause long-term problems with mental health.

## *Amphetamines*

- These are Class-B drugs. They can be prescribed legally by doctors, but if you are found with them and you do not have a prescription, then this is an offence.
- Other names for amphetamines include speed, whiz, dexies and uppers.
- They can be snorted, taken as tablets, smoked or injected.
- Many of the tablets sold are very impure, so it is impossible to know how much amphetamine is actually in them and often difficult to know what the effects will be.

## THE EFFECTS OF AMPHETAMINES

- Amphetamines are stimulants, so they make people feel very excited and 'high'.
- They reduce the appetite, so some people take them if they are trying to lose weight.
- They make the body temperature go up.

## RISKS OF USING AMPHETAMINES

- Most people who use amphetamines regularly become tolerant to them, so they need a larger dose to get the same effect, and easily become addicted.
- They often cause paranoia and hallucinations.
- Because of the problems with purity, some people take unintentional overdoses. These can be fatal.

## *Ecstasy or 'E'*

- Ecstasy is also known as pills or disco biscuits. It is a very popular drug with clubbers.
- It is a Class-A drug, so possession and dealing carry heavy fines and prison sentences.
- Ecstasy is similar to amphetamine and is sometimes called MDMA. Usually it comes as tablets with pictures stamped on them.

### THE EFFECTS OF ECSTASY

- It works by increasing the brain level of a substance called serotonin – and this makes you feel good.
- Users say they have lots of energy, and can keep going all night, and they feel very friendly and affectionate towards everyone.
- Everything feels more intense – especially music and the surroundings.
- The effects can last for several hours.

### RISKS OF USING ECSTASY

- Ecstasy is often contaminated with toxic chemicals.
- Many people say they are selling you 'E' but they may be selling you a dummy tablet that could have serious effects on you – or might have no effect at all. There's no way of knowing!

- There have been deaths reported among people who take ecstasy. Usually, these occur because people take it and then dance for hours and hours, forget to drink and become dehydrated. So if you do take it, it's important to drink little and often. However, you must not drink large amounts of fluid too quickly, because this can cause just as many problems due to over-hydration, which can affect the brain.

## Heroin

- Heroin is sometimes called china white or smack.
- It is a Class-A drug.
- It is made from another drug called morphine, which is extracted from the poppy plant.
- It comes as a powder, which can be smoked or snorted, or dissolved and injected.

### THE EFFECTS OF HEROIN

- It works really quickly – within a few seconds of being taken.
- People say they feel 'high' at first and then start to feel relaxed.

### RISKS OF USING HEROIN

- Heroin causes psychological and physical addiction in many people, so users have to take more and more just to feel normal.
- Many people get into debt to fund their habit, often spending hundreds of pounds per week on the drug.
- As with many drugs, it is often not pure and so the effects can vary widely. This often leads to people taking an accidental overdose if the supply they get is purer than usual.
- Because most people inject heroin, it can cause damage to the veins and skin and lead to blood infections.
- The biggest risks are from viral infections, which are transmitted through blood, such as hepatitis and HIV (see Chapter 6).

- People find it really difficult to deal with a heroin addiction on their own. They usually need help and support from friends and family, and from their GP and local drugs service.

### Rohypnol

- This is a tranquilliser, is also called 'flunitrazepam'.
- It is sometimes known as the 'date rape' drug, because it has been suggested that where it has been put into someone's drink, so that they become drowsy and pass out or experience memory loss, they may have been raped.
- As yet, there have been no proven cases of this happening in the UK, but cases have been brought to court in the USA.

#### THE EFFECTS OF ROHYPNOL

- These are the same as other tranquillisers: the drug reduces feelings of anxiety and leaves someone who takes it feeling very relaxed, and, after a while, quite tired.

#### RISKS OF USING ROHYPNOL OR SIMILAR TRANQUILLISERS

- As well as the possible effects associated with sexual assaults, this is a drug of dependence, and withdrawal of the drug causes nasty side-effects including headaches, muscle pains, tension and severe anxiety.

### GHB

- This is Gammahydroxybutyrate – an anaesthetic drug.
- It is sometimes used by body builders who believe that it allows them to have a really good night's sleep, which will allow the body to build up muscles.
- Sometimes it is described as 'liquid ecstasy' – but in fact it isn't chemically related to ecstasy.
- It is usually sold as a colourless liquid, but it can come in

tablets too. It has been used in some date rapes – people put just a few drops into a drink.

**THE EFFECTS OF GHB**

- GHB slows down body actions.
- If you take a small amount, the effect feels like the effect of having several alcoholic drinks.
- A larger amount causes severe sleepiness and confusion.

**RISKS OF USING GHB**

- High doses can lead to fits and unconsciousness, and eventually to death as you stop breathing.
- Not much is known about longer-term effects, but it may lead to dependence.

## *Anabolic Steroids*

- These are drugs that body builders often use.
- They are related to the male hormone called testosterone, which causes muscle development.
- Some are sold using their trade name – e.g. Durabolin.
- People who use these drugs often call them roids.
- They are Class-C drugs.
- They can be prescribed legally by doctors.
- It is legal to possess them as long as they are for your own use, but someone who supplies them – even if it is just for their friends – could be liable for a fine and prison sentence.

**THE EFFECTS OF ANABOLIC STEROIDS**

- They increase the amount of muscle bulk in the body, so they make people stronger.
- Lots of body builders feel that they make them more determined and allow them to train harder.

**RISKS OF USING ANABOLIC STEROIDS**

- Many people become psychologically dependent on steroids and can feel depressed and tired if they stop taking them.
- Many users also become very aggressive and violent.
- If young people take these pills before they have stopped growing, steroids can actually damage their growth, because they make the growing parts of the bones fuse too early.
- They can eventually cause men to develop breasts and make their testes shrink.
- Female users may develop male features, such as a hairy face.
- Both male and female users may develop acne and fertility problems.
- In the long term, they can cause severe liver and heart problems.

# 6 Life-Threatening Illnesses

**This chapter covers:**

- Cancer
- Epilepsy
- Asthma
- Diabetes
- Anaphylaxis and Severe Allergies
- Meningitis
- Hepatitis
- Appendicitis
- Toxic Shock Syndrome
- AIDS and HIV

This chapter looks at the most common causes of death from serious illness in children and teenagers. After accidents and suicide, cancers are the third most common cause of death in young people. In some cases there is nothing anyone can do to prevent an illness, but in other situations it is more likely that someone can be cured if they have their problem diagnosed early. That's why it's so important to be aware of the warning signs of serious diseases, so you can ask for help or advice as soon as you are worried. Remember, any doctor would far rather be able to reassure you that nothing was wrong than think that you were waiting and worrying in silence.

# Cancer

## WHAT IS IT?

Cancer means an uncontrolled division of abnormal cells in the body. Another name given to many types of cancer is a 'malignant tumour', malignant meaning something that does you harm and tumour meaning a growth, swelling or enlargement. A cancer is usually a lump that grows out of control, often spreading and damaging surrounding tissues. Some cancers stay in one area, but others move through the blood system to other parts of the body.

The most dangerous type of cancer is one that either:

- starts in a vital and difficult-to-reach part of the body, e.g. the brain,
- grows fast, or
- spreads easily.

In these situations, treatment will have less chance of success. However, for any cancer, early detection improves the chance of cure and survival. That's why, although it may be an unpleasant or frightening subject, it is important to know about cancer and be aware of any unexplained change, lump or pain in your body. It probably won't have anything to do with cancer but, if it does, the faster you get help the better your chances. In the UK, about 1,200 people aged up to eighteen are diagnosed with cancer each year.

In general terms we know that eating healthily and taking regular exercise can help reduce the risk of a person's chance of developing cancer.

From time to time, scare stories appear in the media about possible causes of cancers, such as food additives or environmental factors. Generally, these turn out to be untrue.

## SYMPTOMS AND EFFECTS

Each sort of cancer has different symptoms, and this section looks at some of the most common types of cancer in young people. It's very, very important to understand that *all* cancers are rare in young people. And some of the symptoms of cancer are also symptoms of other common conditions that are not at all dangerous. For example, brain tumours can cause headaches – but only a tiny proportion of people with a headache have a brain tumour! They're far more likely to be suffering from stress or a bug such as flu.

## POSSIBLE TREATMENTS

- **Surgery** – to remove the tumour.
- **Chemotherapy** – a series of drugs taken by mouth or injected directly into your veins that targets the cancerous cells.
- **Radiotherapy** – small doses of radiation aimed directly at the tumour to kill the cells.
- **Bone-marrow transplant** – an injection of marrow from the inside of someone else's (the donor's) bone. This can allow the patient's body to make some new healthy white cells.

Treatments for cancer have improved tremendously, and survival rates, particularly for children and young people, have increased a lot. Three out of four young people who develop cancer will now either be completely cured or will go on to live a fairly normal life in spite of their illness.

There are several reasons why young people are now surviving for longer or being cured:

- doctors have learned more about how cancers develop;
- drugs used to treat cancers have become more effective and cause fewer unpleasant side-effects;
- surgical techniques and radiotherapy have improved.

However, about one in every four patients still cannot be cured. In children and teenagers, the most common cancers that kill are brain cancer, leukaemia (cancer of the white blood cells), cancer of the lymph glands such as Hodgkin's disease, and bone cancer.

Even when the cancer can't be cured, modern treatments can prolong life and help make cancer patients much more comfortable during and particularly towards the end of their illness. More than half of young people who die from cancer are cared for by their families at home with the help of specialist nurses and doctors.

There will have to be some hospital visits but these are kept as short as possible, and many hospitals now have special cancer units for young people that are much more informal and cheerful than the old, traditional hospital wards.

## Brain Tumour

### WHAT IS IT?

A brain tumour is a group of cells that starts to develop abnormally in the brain. It can occur anywhere, but in young people is most likely to start around the base of the brain. There are different kinds of tumour depending on the types of cells that are growing out of control. Some are much more serious than others.

### SYMPTOMS AND EFFECTS

Most of the symptoms are due to increased pressure in the brain:

- **headache** – usually severe and intense. Often it's worse when you wake in the morning and gets better later in the day;
- **nausea and vomiting** – often gets worse as the tumour grows. It is different from 'normal' vomiting, which happens when

you have a stomach bug or food poisoning, as it is not usually associated with any abdominal pain;

- **double or blurred vision** – a sign of increasing pressure on the nerves at the back of the eye.

**POSSIBLE TREATMENTS**

Neurosurgery (brain surgery) is often necessary. Sometimes the tumour is too big to remove safely, so a smaller operation, to remove the easily reached part of the tumour, is combined with radiotherapy or chemotherapy.

## *Leukaemia*

**WHAT IS IT?**

Leukaemia is a cancer of the white blood cells, which are produced in the bone marrow. Bone marrow is a spongy material found inside long bones, such as the thighbone, and it produces the cells that develop into the three different types of blood cells:

- red blood cells, which carry oxygen around the body;
- white blood cells, which fight infections;
- platelets, which make the blood sticky and help it to clot so that bleeding can be controlled.

In leukaemia, the bone marrow makes large numbers of abnormal white cells but not enough red blood cells or platelets.

The commonest type of leukaemia in children and young people is called acute lymphoblastic leukaemia. There are about four hundred and fifty cases in England and Wales each year.

**SYMPTOMS AND EFFECTS**

Because there are fewer red blood cells in circulation, the patient with leukaemia becomes anaemic. They look pale and become easily tired and breathless, as not enough oxygen is being carried around their body. The reduced level of platelets means that the blood doesn't clot very efficiently and bleeding or bruising may be visible under the skin. The white cells that are being produced are not fully developed, and they don't work as well as they should to fight infections. One of the dangers of leukaemia is that patients often get serious infections like pneumonia (a lung infection).

**POSSIBLE TREATMENTS**

The treatment for leukaemia is usually chemotherapy. A series of different drugs is used in cycles of treatment over a period of about two years. In some cases, bone marrow transplants are also used. Because a leukaemia patient is very vulnerable to infection, they may have to stay in hospital quite a lot and at times – e.g. after a bone marrow transplant – may have to stay in isolation so they are not at risk of infection from other patients or visitors. Most children and young people now survive the disease – the cure rate is about eighty per cent.

## Sophie's Story

I was only six when I first had leukaemia. I suddenly started to get really tired at school. I can remember falling asleep at my desk when we were supposed to be writing a story. The same thing happened again later that week. At first, my teacher was a bit cross, but then she had a word with my mum, who said I was tired at home too, which just wasn't like me. A couple of days later, I woke up in the morning with three big bruises on my legs – and didn't have a clue as to why they had appeared. Mum took me straight to the doctor who did a blood test and rang my parents later that day to say I needed to go to hospital.

The doctors in the hospital were really nice, but they did lots of tests that were quite painful. I had some fluid taken out of my back (they called the test a lumbar puncture) and a needle in the breastbone so they could look at my bone marrow. Luckily, I went to sleep for that test! I had lots of drugs, which they gave me through a drip, and I also had to have drugs in the form of pills. I was on treatment for two years, and they carried on seeing me and doing blood tests for the next three years.

Now I'm nearly twelve and I seem to be cured – so I feel like I'm one of the lucky ones. I missed a lot of school because of the treatment, and even though there was a school in the hospital, I often felt too tired and sick, because of the drugs, to concentrate on work. So I'm trying hard to catch up now, and my school has been great at helping me.

When you're in hospital you meet lots of patients with the same illness. I became great friends with Gemma, who was the same age as me. She had a really bad time – about a year into her treatment the leukaemia got worse and she had to have a special treatment called a bone marrow transplant. This is where they get some 'good' bone marrow from someone in your family, or someone else with matching cells, and inject it into you. Poor Gemma was in hospital for ages, and for a long time was in a room on her own, and all her visitors had to wear gowns and masks to stop her catching any bugs. Her older brother gave her some of his bone marrow – so he ended up in hospital for a few days too. I saw Gemma a couple of weeks ago and she looked really fit for the first time in ages, so I'm keeping my fingers crossed that the treatment will work.

Sophie, 11

## *Hodgkin's Disease*

### WHAT IS IT?

This is a cancer that affects the lymphatic system. The lymphatic system is the body's defence against infection, and it is made up of lymph glands (nodes) connected to each other by tiny vessels. You may have felt enlarged lymph glands in your neck when you have had a sore throat. When the body comes across any infection, the glands get bigger and produce more white cells, which help to fight that infection. There are glands all over the body – in the neck, the armpits, chest, abdomen and in the groin at the top of the legs.

## SYMPTOMS AND EFFECTS

The first sign is usually a painless swelling in a gland. Often, the glands in the neck are affected first. If glands swell up because of an infection, they usually feel quite tender when you touch them. In Hodgkin's disease, however, they are usually painless. Glands all over the body can be affected. If those in the chest are affected, then the person can get a nasty cough or become breathless. Many people with Hodgkin's disease get high fevers, especially at night, and some lose weight – even though they may be eating normally.

In order to make the diagnosis, doctors will remove a part of a lymph gland, so that they can look at the cells under a microscope. They will arrange for scans, X-rays and blood tests, so that they can see how far the disease has spread. This is called 'staging' the disease – and it is done so that the best treatment can be given.

## POSSIBLE TREATMENTS

Treatment mainly involves chemotherapy. In some cases, radio-therapy is needed too. The good news is that about ninety per cent of cases are curable.

# Alex's Story

I was in the middle of my Key Stage 3 SATs tests last summer when I started to feel absolutely tired out all the time. I was really worried about how I was going to do in the tests – I wanted to be in the same maths set as my best friend and knew that was going to be difficult to achieve. So at first, when I told my mum how awful I felt, she said it was probably just my nerves. But one morning a couple of weeks after I started to feel unwell, I was putting my silver chain around my neck, and I noticed that it was tighter than usual – and when I looked in the mirror, I could see that my neck was swollen on one side. Mum thought I must have tonsillitis, so she got me to 'open wide' and show her my throat. It was fine – and my throat wasn't sore anyway. I waited a couple of days to see if the swelling would go, but it didn't, and the next thing I noticed was a lump under my arm. Again it was completely painless. It felt about as big as a large marble. It was all rubbery feeling, and the skin over the top seemed to be stuck to the lump. I also realised that for the last few days, when I woke up each morning, my sheets were really damp and sticky – I'd been sweating so much. When I told Mum all this, she looked really anxious and arranged for me to see the doctor that day. After a trip to the hospital, I found out that I had Hodgkin's disease. I was told that it was the second most common type of cancer in people of my age – after leukaemia. The doctor explained all the treatment to me and said that I should do well as the cancer only seemed to be affecting the two areas – my neck and under my arm. Treatment lasted for months, and made me feel even more tired. I ended up missing a lot of time from school, and although I got some help from a tutor who came to the house I decided in the end to repeat the first year of my GCSE courses. I'm now back at school full time and concentrating on staying well and getting on with life.

Alex, 16

## Bone Cancer
### WHAT IS IT?

Bone cancer is a malignant tumour that grows in a bone. It is slightly more common in young men than young women. It can affect any bone in the body, but is most common in the arms, legs and pelvis.

## SYMPTOMS AND EFFECTS

The main symptom is pain around the affected area. This may start as an ache that won't go away and often feels worse at night. After a while there may be some swelling and the area becomes uncomfortable or painful to touch. In young people the symptoms are sometimes mistaken for 'growing pains'. However, growing pains (odd fleeting pains that seem to occur mainly during peak periods of growth) tend to come and go and move around the body. Any pain that stays in one place – and particularly if it's in one arm or one leg as opposed to both – should always be investigated.

Sometimes there are no symptoms at all until the person breaks a bone playing sport or after a minor fall. An X-ray might show that the bone has already been weakened by the cancer.

As with most cancers, as it gets worse, a person will become more tired and will probably lose weight.

## POSSIBLE TREATMENTS

A combination of treatments is usually necessary for bone cancer. Chemotherapy is often used first to try to shrink the tumour, then surgery may be necessary to remove it. Sometimes this means removing part of a bone or even, if the cancer is well advanced, part of a limb. Obviously, surgeons would be reluctant to do this unless it was absolutely necessary and different options for reconstruction would be explained. In some cases, depending on the particular type of bone cancer, radiotherapy is used instead of surgery.

## *Other Bone Tumours*

Not all bony lumps are cancerous (malignant). Some are called benign tumours. These are lumps that do not spread. However, because they can cause pain and may weaken the bone, leading to fractures or breaks, they are usually removed by surgery.

## *Malignant Melanoma*
### WHAT IS IT?

Malignant melanoma is a dangerous form of skin cancer – the main cause of this is skin damage from sunburn. This is one disease that is definitely on the increase, and in the UK there are around 6,000 new cases of malignant melanoma each year. People with fair skin or freckles who burn easily are at greatest risk of skin cancer. Malignant melanoma affects women more than men and tends to be more common in young people. There seems to be a strong link between sunburn in young people and skin cancer, so getting red and burned as a child or teenager can increase your risk of developing malignant melanoma later in life.

### SYMPTOMS AND EFFECTS

Malignant melanoma can develop anywhere on the body. Usually, either a new dark mole appears or an existing mole starts to change shape, size or colour. It may develop irregular edges or bleed or get itchy. If you notice any of these changes, you should see your doctor as soon as possible. This is a fast-growing cancer, so it is important to have treatment early.

### PREVENTION OF MALIGNANT MELANOMA

You can reduce the chances of getting this type of skin cancer by avoiding too much sun exposure and sunburn by:

- keeping out of the midday sun, i.e. between 11 a.m. and 3 p.m. – stay in the shade instead;
- covering up as much skin as possible – wear a hat, a shirt and some loose trousers if you have fair skin;

- using a high-factor sun protection skin cream, at least SPF15, regularly throughout the day and remember especially to keep applying more after swimming;
- NOT using sunbeds.

**POSSIBLE TREATMENTS**

Treatment may include surgical removal, chemotherapy and radiotherapy. Sadly, malignant melanomas often spread to the liver or bones and can be fatal. The earlier they are treated, the better the chance of survival, so keep an eye on your moles, look out for any new ones and ask your doctor's opinion if you are worried.

## Testicular Cancer

**WHAT IS IT?**

This is a tumour that grows in one of the testes or 'balls'. It is the most common cancer to affect men between nineteen and forty-four, but it also accounts for three per cent of cases of cancer in fifteen- to twenty-four-year-old men.

It is important to examine your testes every month. The easiest time to do this is in the bath or shower, so that the scrotum (the sac containing the testes) is relaxed. Use your fingers and thumbs to check their shape, size and feel. Try to notice whether they have become harder or less smooth than usual.

**SYMPTOMS AND EFFECTS**

You may discover that one testis becomes bigger than the other, or you may find a lump. Many people get a dull aching feeling in the groin. Don't ignore any changes – they could be caused by many things apart from cancer, but it's still important to get them checked out straight away. If it does turn out to be cancer, the sooner you get treatment, the more likely you are to be cured.

**POSSIBLE TREATMENTS**

These depend on whether the cancer has spread anywhere else. The affected testicle is usually removed, and you may be given chemotherapy, and possibly radiotherapy, as well.

## *Breast Cancer*

Many young people worry about breast cancer, particularly if they have a relative such as a mum or gran who has had it. However, it is extremely rare in young people. If you do find a lump in your breast, it is most likely to be due to either fluid retention – which gets worse before your period – or a fibroadenoma – a harmless piece of tissue. If you are at all worried, you should ask your practice nurse or a GP to check any lump for you.

# Epilepsy

**WHAT IS IT?**

Epilepsy is a condition where someone has a series of seizures or fits. It affects about one in a hundred and thirty people in the UK, but many more people than this – about one in twenty – will have a fit at some time in their lives. The most common sort of fit is a 'febrile convulsion' – a fit that occurs in a young child when they have a high temperature. This may happen once or twice but on its own does not mean that the child has epilepsy. Epilepsy is caused by sudden outbursts of electro-chemical activity in one area of the brain. This interferes with the normal messages that the brain is constantly sending to and receiving from all parts of the body. Someone is usually described as suffering from epilepsy only when they have had several fits and when a brain-wave test shows a typical electrical pattern.

**SYMPTOMS AND EFFECTS**

There are many types of seizures. The classic type of epilepsy, which most people would recognise, is the 'grand mal' fit. This is where the person becomes unconscious and then has jerky movements of their arms and legs – first going stiff and then shaking. Often, they bite their tongue and they may lose control of their bladder and wet themselves.

Another common type is the 'petit mal' seizure, where the person looks as if they are daydreaming for a few seconds. This type is quite common in young people, and it can mean that they are missing quite a lot of information, e.g. they just don't hear whole sentences when a teacher is talking. Sometimes petit mal epilepsy comes to light only when a child is in trouble at school for 'not paying attention'.

More unusual types of epilepsy include 'temporal lobe' epilepsy, where the person may hear or smell unusual things, and 'frontal lobe' epilepsy, where they may have dramatic mood changes.

Some people can recognise common things that will trigger a seizure for them. This might be a high fever, stress, bright or flashing lights, hunger or some kinds of drugs. They may have a few seconds' warning before the seizure starts.

## Steve's Story

I remember the first time I had a fit very clearly. I was ten and had been out for the day with my dad – we went to watch United play, and I really enjoyed the game. Afterwards, I started to feel a bit sick and dizzy as we were walking back to the car park. The next thing I knew, I was lying on my side on the ground, and I felt absolutely awful – I had a splitting headache and felt heavy all over. My dad looked absolutely terrified – he told me to lie still and that an ambulance was on its way. The rest of the evening is a bit of a blur –

I heard that I was taken to the casualty department and the doctors there had a good look at me and told Dad that it sounded as though I had had a fit. Apparently, I was shaking all over and I actually wet myself. I wasn't put on any treatment then; they just arranged for me to have a brain-wave test (EEG) about four weeks later. The test showed that I might have more fits, and in fact I did have another one about six weeks later. I went to see a paediatrician (a specialist in children's illnesses), and she said it would be better for me to take some medicine every day to try to stop another fit happening. That was fine by me – I felt really embarrassed at the thought of having another fit in front of my friends – so I started to take medicine twice each day. I've tried to stop the medicine a couple of times, but each time I do the fits come back. I'm fourteen now and just hope I might grow out of the fits soon – my doctor says there is a good chance that might happen. I know that if I get really hungry or tired I am more likely to have a fit – so nowadays I make sure I get plenty of sleep and look after myself.

Steve, 14

There is a syndrome called 'sudden death in epilepsy' (SUDEP) in which people die unexpectedly after a seizure. However, most of the 1,000 deaths per year associated with epilepsy are due to an accident associated with a fit. For this reason you should never take part in dangerous sports or activities on your own. People with well-controlled epilepsy are extremely unlikely to die from it.

**HOW TO TELL THE DIFFERENCE BETWEEN A FIT AND A FAINT**
A faint is due to a temporary decrease of oxygen supply to the brain. This is caused either by a fall in blood pressure – which can happen when someone stands up for a long time (e.g. if a student stands up in assembly for an hour on a hot day, so the

blood pools in the feet) – or the effect of a sudden fright or shock, or when someone gets dehydrated or misses a meal.

In a faint the person may feel:

- sick and dizzy;
- hot and cold;
- sweaty and clammy.

And then they fall to the floor.

While they're on the floor, the lack of oxygen to the brain may mean that they have a couple of jerky movements, and this can look like someone having a fit. In fact, there is a special name for this – a 'reflex anoxic seizure'. This is NOT a form of epilepsy, and people who have faints like this are no more likely than anyone else to go on to get 'true' epilepsy.

About a minute after someone has fainted, they start to come round and they can usually get up after a few minutes.

In a grand mal epileptic fit, which is due to an electrical disturbance in the brain, the person usually doesn't have much warning. They can have a fit at any time – walking, standing, sitting or lying down. They will suddenly fall to the floor, go stiff and then start to shake, possibly losing control of their bladder as well. They may produce a lot of saliva, so they seem to froth at the mouth, and can make gurgling sounds in their throat. When they come round, they'll probably feel very tired and they may sleep for several hours afterwards.

**POSSIBLE TREATMENTS**

Most people who have fits are seen by a hospital doctor who will organise some tests. These include an electro-encephalogram (EEG) – or brain-wave test, and in some cases a brain scan.

Most people with epilepsy are perfectly healthy and often

there's no obvious cause for the fits. Sometimes tests might suggest that there was brain damage at birth or show damage caused by a previous head injury or severe infection or brain tumour.

In a few people with very severe epilepsy, complicated brain surgery has helped to decrease the number of fits they have. However, most people are treated with drugs. Sometimes these can have side-effects such as making patients feel sleepy or gain weight, so anyone who is given drugs for epilepsy should be monitored carefully.

Many young people seem to 'grow out' of epilepsy, and that's why doctors will try to reduce gradually the amount of medication while keeping an eye on their patients to make sure that the fits do not return.

If you do have epilepsy, there are several things that you need to do or be aware of:

- Tell your friends and teachers that you have epilepsy so that they will know what to do if you suddenly have a fit. This may be difficult for you, and some people mistakenly think that people who have fits must have some sort of learning difficulty. But by being matter of fact and explaining that your epilepsy is only a very small part of who you are, you can help overcome their prejudices.
- You shouldn't go swimming, climbing or bike riding on your own.
- Be aware that anti-epileptic drugs can interact with other medicines such as the contraceptive pill. If you need to take any other drugs, you should discuss it with your doctor or the pharmacist first.
- Alcohol and drugs such as cocaine can also have a very different and dangerous effect on people who have epilepsy.

**WHAT TO DO IF SOMEONE YOU ARE WITH HAS A SEIZURE**

- Help them into the recovery position – lying on their side with the uppermost arm and leg stretched out to stop them rolling on to their face. (See Chapter 9 for diagram.)
- Do not put anything in their mouth. It is better for them to bite their tongue than for them to damage their teeth on a hard piece of wood!
- If this is the first fit they have had, or if it lasts more than ten minutes, get someone to call for an ambulance. They may need oxygen and a drug to help stop the fit.
- Check to see if they have a Medic Alert bracelet, which may tell you the type of medication or treatment they will need.

# Asthma

**WHAT IS IT?**

Asthma is a condition where the lining of the air passageways in the lungs becomes swollen, making them very narrow, causing difficulty in breathing. When someone has asthma, they may have noisy breathing and breathe more quickly than usual.

Around one in eight children in the UK has asthma. About seventy-five per cent will grow out of it in adolescence and never have another attack. Others will be free from problems for many years – often until they're in middle age. Some people have asthma all their lives.

You're more likely to have asthma if one of your parents or a brother or sister has it. Some people get their first attack when they have a nasty chest infection. Other people develop an allergy (sensitivity), usually to something in the air. Common causes of allergy are house-dust mites (minute bugs that live in mattresses and carpets), feathers (e.g. in pillows and duvets), pollen (from grass and other plants) and cat and dog fur. Some people are allergic to several different things.

Once someone has one asthma attack, they seem to become more sensitive to whatever the particular triggers are for them. In some young people, going out from a warm house into the cold air can cause an attack. Other people find that they get wheezy when they exercise.

### SYMPTOMS AND EFFECTS

Although about 1,500 people in the UK die from asthma each year, most of the deaths are in adults or in people who have not been taking the treatment prescribed by their doctor. Some people just hadn't realised how sick they were.

### SYMPTOMS OF A MILD ASTHMA ATTACK

Symptoms usually start with coughing and a feeling of tightness in the chest. The typical symptom is the wheeze. This is a whistling sound when you breathe, and it's a sign that your airways are narrowed. This means you should have some treatment.

### SYMPTOMS OF A SEVERE ASTHMA ATTACK

In a severe asthma attack, the person finds it more and more difficult to breathe. You might notice them clenching up all the muscles in their chest and neck in an effort to open up their lungs. They probably can't talk, because they're too breathless, and their nostrils may flare open as they try to breathe in through their nose. Their heartbeat gets very fast, and eventually they may go blue and find it difficult to stand up or walk around. If this happens, it is an emergency and you must get the person to the GP or an A and E department straight away. If you go to A and E or take someone else there, it is important to let the doctors know what medication you or they have had already.

**POSSIBLE TREATMENTS**

People who have lots of asthma attacks usually take two drugs most of the time. These are often both given via an inhaler or 'puffer'. They are a broncho-dilator (called a 'reliever') and a steroid inhaler (called a 'preventer'). In severe cases, where a patient still has lots of attacks, other drugs may also be prescribed.

The usual treatment for people with mild, occasional asthma is an inhaler, which helps to get a broncho-dilator drug into the lungs. This helps widen the narrow passageways and relieves the symptoms. It's important for people to follow the instructions on the package very carefully. Many people don't take this medication properly and then it doesn't work. Taking too much can cause side-effects like a racing heart rate. If the medication doesn't help the symptoms or the wheezing is getting worse, a different type of treatment may be needed to prevent a severe attack.

If a person is taken to the GP or hospital with a severe attack, they will be given a broncho-dilator drug (often through a machine called a nebuliser, which is easier to use than an inhaler) and they will probably be given another type of drug – a steroid – usually by injection. They will also be given oxygen.

The doctors will try to find out if anything caused the attack, such as a chest infection or an allergy to something. After a bad episode or if someone has several trips to A and E in a short space of time, doctors may prescribe a short course of steroid tablets. These help reduce the inflammation in the airways.

## Nick's Story

My mum told me that I used to get asthma when I was a baby – but I can't remember anything about it. When I was twelve I had a bad cold and cough, and after a couple of days my chest felt funny. It was hard to take a big enough breath in so I was having to breathe more often. I went for a walk just to the local shop but got really tired, and my chest felt tight. Mum took me to the GP that evening. He had a good listen to my chest and told me it was wheezy, which meant I had asthma. He gave me an inhaler to use and showed me how to get the drug in the inhaler into my lungs. The inhaler was meant to make the air passages wider – he called it a broncho-dilator. It worked really well – I could feel my chest getting better straight away. He told me I had probably got wheezy because of the cold, but that other things could start off an asthma attack. Over the next few months, I had more attacks – often when I was playing football or if I went outside on a very cold day. The doctor suggested that I should have another type of inhaler to use twice each day to try to prevent the attacks from happening. This was a steroid inhaler. He explained that it worked by calming the airways down. I might still need to use the first inhaler as well, if I got an attack. Since then I have felt fine. I go for a check-up with the asthma nurse at the doctor's surgery every three months and she checks to see if my lungs are working OK. I know lots of people have more problems with their asthma than I do, so I feel quite lucky. I hope it might just stop again in the future, but I know that it could get worse and I could get attacks if I develop any allergies. We have a cat and a dog in the house, and they don't cause any problems for me – I hope things stay like that.

*Nick, 14*

# Diabetes

**WHAT IS IT?**

Diabetes is a condition where you have a problem dealing with sugar in the bloodstream. Sugar is produced when the body burns up food. It is important to have a certain level of sugar in the blood, as it's the best and most quickly available form of energy to keep your body going. If the level gets too low, it makes you feel weak and floppy and sometimes sweaty and faint. You may have noticed this happening sometimes if you don't eat for several hours.

In diabetes, the blood-sugar level is generally too high. A person who is diabetic will then lose some sugar in their urine. This is one of the tests that doctors use if they think someone might be diabetic. The reason that the sugar level is high is that the person either doesn't have enough insulin or the insulin doesn't work properly.

Insulin is a hormone produced in the pancreas, a small gland that lies behind the stomach. Insulin helps keep the level of sugar in the blood constant. If there isn't enough insulin, the level of blood sugar just keeps on rising.

**SYMPTOMS AND EFFECTS**

In the short term, a quick rise in sugar can make someone with diabetes get ill very quickly. The body tries to get rid of the extra sugar in the urine, so someone with diabetes tends to get very thirsty and may want to drink more often – including in the night. Even though there is a lot of sugar in the bloodstream, the body can't store it to use throughout the day, so patients feel tired and hungry. Because the body isn't able to use up the energy from food it will start to burn up its own fat. The person loses weight, and chemicals called ketones appear in the blood. These can lead to drowsiness and eventually to diabetic coma. If you or someone you know develops these symptoms, it is important to see a doctor straight away.

Every year a small number of young people die from diabetes – either because it wasn't diagnosed in time for any treatment to be effective or because they didn't realise how seriously ill they could become and didn't take their medication. If someone has an infection, their blood-sugar control can be badly affected. This is another time when it is important to check things out with a doctor.

**POSSIBLE TREATMENTS**

Treatment depends on the type of diabetes that a patient has. There are two types of diabetes. Type I is the most common in children and young people. In this condition the pancreas gland stops making insulin and there is no treatment to make it start to produce any more. Patients with Type I diabetes need insulin treatment, several times a day, for the rest of their lives. At the moment this is given by injection, and children as young as seven learn to give their own injections. The amount of insulin they need is calculated by monitoring the sugar levels in the blood with a simple blood test. Scientists are trying to develop other ways for insulin to be given, e.g. via a nasal spray.

The other type of diabetes is called Type II. It used to be seen only in old people who were very overweight, as increased body fat affects the ability of the pancreas to produce enough insulin, but Type II diabetes is now appearing in some children and young people who are severely overweight. Doctors are very worried about what will happen in the future, as we know that the problem of obesity in childhood is getting worse very fast. The health of some people with Type II diabetes can improve if they lose weight, but some need diabetic drugs or even insulin injections. The best way of preventing Type II diabetes is to keep your weight within normal limits for your height and age – and to take regular exercise.

# Kirsty's Story

Diabetes was something I had heard about because my gran has it. She is really fat and quite old, so I thought diabetes was something that only people like her got! I was usually very healthy, but over one weekend last year I started to feel a bit strange. The first thing that happened was that I kept waking up in the night to go to the loo for a wee. I know some people do that once in the night – but this was every couple of hours. I felt incredibly thirsty, so I started drinking lots more water. Mum said that I shouldn't drink so much – that must be why I needed the loo all the time. But I just got thirstier and thirstier. By the Sunday night I felt all weak and floppy. When I put my school skirt on the next day, Mum noticed that I had lost some weight – and I honestly hadn't been trying to diet. I started to feel very sick and dizzy, so Mum called the NHS Direct helpline to see if they thought I needed to see my doctor. They said it sounded like I should have a urine test to look for sugar, so we went to the surgery later that day. The test was positive, and I was sent straight up to the Children's Centre at the local hospital. I had blood tests there, and the doctors explained that I had `insulin dependent' diabetes. I was really fed up to learn that I would have to give myself insulin injections and take care with my diet. In fact, it was much easier to deal with than I imagined. I was only in hospital for the one day, and now I have two insulin injections each day and check my blood-sugar levels before meals. I know that if I stick to the diet – which is really just a healthy-eating programme – I should be fine. I've heard that they are working on a way of giving insulin without injections – that would be great.

Kirsty, 12

# Anaphylaxis and Severe Allergies

## WHAT ARE THEY?

Lots of people are allergic to something, such as dust, pollen from grass or trees, or a particular food. Most people get symptoms like a runny nose, itchy red eyes or a slight wheeze if they come into contact with the thing they are allergic to – the allergen. If the substance is a food, they may get a stomach ache or diarrhoea. These symptoms are usually easily dealt with by using an antihistamine cream or taking tablets, such as hay fever medication. In a few people, the first reaction to a substance can be quite mild but the next time the person comes into contact with the substance the reaction could be much worse. A few people develop a really severe form of allergy, called an anaphylactic reaction. Every year a few young people die because of an anaphylactic reaction.

## SYMPTOMS AND EFFECTS

The reaction usually starts almost immediately after the allergen has been eaten, inhaled, or has come into contact with the skin. Most of the time the reaction is caused by a very tiny amount of an allergen. Common causes are peanuts, wasp stings and shellfish. A few people are allergic to certain drugs such as penicillin. The patient may get a swollen face, lip and throat swelling, and will often start to wheeze. They may notice that their heart is beating really fast. In some cases they may become unconscious and collapse.

## POSSIBLE TREATMENTS

The most important thing is to avoid the substance that has caused a severe reaction. People who are allergic to nuts, for example, need to take great care with everything that they eat –

because nuts are added to lots of foods like cakes and biscuits and lots of sweets.

Anyone who has had a severe reaction will be referred to their local hospital to see an allergy specialist. They may do some skin tests or blood tests to check if the person has any other allergies. They usually give the patient a special injection device that contains a drug called adrenalin. It looks like a pen, and can be given by the patient themselves or by a friend or relative who is with them. The injection can even be given through clothes, so you don't have to waste any time. Anyone with a severe allergy should wear a special-alert bracelet and make sure that their friends and teachers at school or college know about the problem. In most schools, the school nurse will go into school and train several of the teachers so that any of them could help out if the young person had a reaction at school. Peanut allergy in particular seems to be getting more common – some people are so allergic that they would have a dangerous reaction even if they just inhaled some peanut dust.

# Meningitis

**WHAT IS IT?**

Meningitis is a serious infection caused by a virus or bacteria. It can come on extremely suddenly and causes inflammation of the covering of the brain and spinal cord, making a person very ill very fast.

Meningitis can occur at any age, but bacterial meningitis is more common in children, while viral meningitis is more common in young adults.

Vaccination protects people from some – but not all – forms of meningitis. It is therefore extremely important to get medical help if you think you or a friend may have this disease.

## SYMPTOMS AND EFFECTS

Often, the illness starts like flu with a high temperature and headache and sore, aching muscles.

Someone with bacterial meningitis will get worse very fast, often over just a few hours. The symptoms of viral meningitis may take several days to develop. The symptoms of either type include some or all of the following:

- severe headache;
- fever;
- stiff neck;
- dislike of bright lights;
- feeling sick or vomiting.

## THE GLASS TEST

In a severe form of meningitis (meningococcal meningitis) a rash may develop that starts as purple-red pinprick spots and quickly spreads to become big, dark red blotches. This is a complication of the infection called septicaemia. The rash does not fade if pressed. You can test this by pressing the side of a glass against the blotchy patches. Look at the skin through the glass and see whether pressing on it reduces the redness. If a person is just flushed and hot or feverish, the redness will disappear and the skin will go very pale as you press. If the skin stays purple or red and blotchy, then there is a strong chance the person has meningococcal septicaemia.

Get help **FAST**, i.e. go to a hospital A and E department.

For more information, look at *www.meningitis.org* and go to the section on symptoms.

## POSSIBLE TREATMENTS

Immediate hospital medical treatment is needed if meningitis is suspected. Meningitis can kill and, because it can strike so fast, delaying treatment by even an hour or two can affect whether someone lives or dies.

Treatment includes antibiotics and other powerful drugs.

## Jenny's Story

I was the sort of person who was never ill, so when I started feeling a bit shivery and shaky one morning in my maths lesson I didn't take too much notice. But after about half an hour I felt very strange. My joints were really sore and I had a splitting headache. By lunchtime I was much worse, and I was throwing up even though I hadn't eaten anything all day. My best friend practically dragged me along to the school office, although I just wanted to curl up in a corner and go to sleep. Our secretary at school has done some first aid, so she asked me a few questions and had a look at my arms and legs, though I wasn't sure what she was looking for. Then she insisted on ringing my mum at work so she could collect me and take me to the doctor's.

When we got to the GP surgery, the receptionist saw that I looked awful and sent me straight in to see the doctor. He made me bend my neck and that was really sore. He also had another look at my arms, and I was surprised to see that by now tiny red spots had appeared. He pressed hard on my arm using a drinking glass – and showed me that, instead of fading away, the spots still looked red even through the glass pressed against them. He told Mum that he was very worried about me and wanted to send me straight into the hospital – by ambulance!

Before the ambulance came, he gave me an injection into my thigh – he said it was penicillin – and it stung a lot. After that, I don't remember very much. I started feeling a bit floppy and thought that people's voices were coming from a long way away. The next thing I knew I was waking up in a noisy intensive-care unit – hooked up to about ten machines. My parents were looking really worried, and when my mum saw that my eyes were open she burst into tears.

Gradually, they told me what had happened. When I got to the hospital I was unconscious, and tests showed that I had meningococcal septicaemia – there were bacteria in my bloodstream. I was told that my school secretary and doctor had probably saved my life by making sure I got good medical attention so quickly. While I was in intensive care, my kidneys had stopped working properly so I had a treatment called dialysis. This means that the blood is taken away from the body and toxins (poisons) are removed before the blood is returned.

Overall, I was in hospital for ten days and felt really wobbly for about four weeks afterwards. Everyone who had been in close contact with me was given some antibiotics to try to prevent them from getting the disease. Luckily, all my friends and family were fine. I heard later that someone from a nearby town had died from the same illness a couple of weeks before I was admitted to hospital. That makes me feel that I was one of the lucky ones.

I've now learned how to do the glass test myself and would recommend everyone to take a couple of minutes to learn how to do it. I really believe it saved my life!

Jenny, 15

# Hepatitis

**WHAT IS IT?**

Hepatitis literally means 'inflammation of the liver'. As one of the largest organs in the body, the liver has several very important functions, including:

- producing enzymes that help to process digested food;
- controlling levels of nutrients in the blood;
- fighting and destroying toxins (poisonous substances).

135

If your liver is damaged or inflamed, it can't work properly and you can feel very ill indeed.

Most cases of hepatitis are caused by infection with a virus, and the three main viruses are known as hepatitis A, B and C. These are passed on in different ways and can cause different symptoms.

Some cases of hepatitis are caused by other illnesses like glandular fever or by drinking too much alcohol or exposure to some drugs and chemicals.

### SYMPTOMS AND EFFECTS

**Hepatitis A** is passed from person to person by eating food or drinking water contaminated with the virus or through poor personal hygiene, e.g. not washing your hands after going to the toilet. It tends to cause tiredness, aches and pains, a high temperature, loss of appetite, nausea, vomiting, stomach ache and diarrhoea. You may notice your skin and the whites of your eyes turning yellow. This is a sign of jaundice and means that your liver is not functioning properly.

However, hepatitis A does not usually cause long-term liver damage. A vaccine is available, and people who are travelling to 'high-risk' countries should make sure they have it before they leave.

**Hepatitis B** is transmitted through blood and other body fluids, so it can be passed on during unprotected sex or via contaminated needles. Sometimes it doesn't cause any symptoms at all for six months, but then jaundice, tiredness and loss of appetite are common.

Sometimes people recover, but others can go on to develop a liver disease called cirrhosis, which means scarring of the liver. This can eventually kill them. A vaccine is available to protect people from hepatitis B, and particular groups who are at higher risk of getting the disease, such as health workers who could get injuries from needles and in the operating theatre, are offered vaccination.

**Hepatitis C** is also passed on through infected blood. It is becoming more common, and many people don't know they have the infection until years later when they get liver cirrhosis. There is no vaccine for this form of hepatitis.

POSSIBLE TREATMENTS

If hepatitis is suspected, a doctor will take blood tests to check liver function and to look for antibodies to the different hepatitis viruses.

If the illness is caused by exposure to drugs or chemicals, it may be possible to give an antidote to help the liver recover. In some cases caused by viruses, special anti-viral treatments are being developed. Otherwise there is no specific treatment for hepatitis apart from rest and a good diet. Unless serious damage has occurred, people usually recover in a few weeks. However, the liver's ability to produce the enzymes needed to metabolise alcohol is damaged by an attack of hepatitis and, in turn, taking alcohol can damage a liver that is already inflamed. For this reason, people who have had any type of hepatitis are usually advised not to drink alcohol for at least a year.

# Appendicitis

WHAT IS IT?

The appendix is a small piece of gut (like a worm) in the abdomen. It can become red and inflamed due to infection, and this condition is called appendicitis.

**SYMPTOMS AND EFFECTS**

Most people start off with abdominal (tummy) pain. It often begins around the umbilicus (tummy button) and it can make you feel sick and lose your appetite. You might then develop a high temperature.

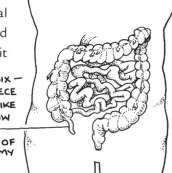

THE APPENDIX — A SMALL PIECE OF WORM-LIKE GUT – BELOW AND TO THE RIGHT OF YOUR TUMMY BUTTON

The pain gets worse and usually moves to the right side of the abdomen – below and to the right of the umbilicus, where it first started. When the painful area is pressed, it is very sore.

If the problem is not diagnosed, then the appendix can burst, releasing pus into the abdomen – and this can (rarely) be fatal.

**POSSIBLE TREATMENTS**

Treatment involves surgery – the appendix is removed. People usually get better in a few days, and as the appendix isn't used for anything there are rarely any problems after surgery.

# Toxic Shock Syndrome

**WHAT IS IT?**

Toxic shock syndrome (TSS) is an extremely rare but serious illness caused by an overwhelming infection that affects mainly girls. In about half the cases it is associated with using a tampon. It is a reaction to toxins (poisons) produced by a bacterial infection.

**SYMPTOMS AND EFFECTS**

Symptoms can include:

- a flu-like illness;
- high temperature;
- vomiting and/or diarrhoea;
- sore throat;
- dizziness;
- fainting;
- a blotchy rash (like severe sunburn).

**POSSIBLE TREATMENTS**

This illness needs emergency treatment in hospital. If you have the symptoms listed above, do tell the doctors if you have been using tampons and remove your tampon immediately.

You will be less at risk of TSS if you:

- never use tampons or use them only on the heaviest days of a period;
- change tampons frequently;
- always remember to remove the last tampon at the end of a period.

TSS can be successfully treated with antibiotics if it is diagnosed early enough.

# AIDS and HIV

**WHAT ARE THEY?**

AIDS stands for acquired immune deficiency syndrome. It is caused by infection from a virus called the HIV virus (human immunodeficiency virus). This virus attacks the immune system –

the parts of your body (white blood cells and glands) that fights any infection and diseases. Infection with HIV is usually caused by having unprotected sex with someone who carries the HIV virus. This person may not be ill at the time, as the virus can lie dormant for a while. In the past some people became infected through having blood transfusions – if the original blood donor was HIV positive. Now all blood is screened in the UK and developed countries, so this should never happen. Some babies catch the virus from their mother, so now pregnant women are screened and the baby can be treated for the disease very soon after birth. It is also possible to catch HIV from dirty needles, so it is much more common among drug addicts.

The only way to protect yourself from HIV is to avoid infection. This means either not having sex or always using a condom. Drug users should never share needles.

## SYMPTOMS AND EFFECTS OF HIV

Often, HIV causes an illness like flu, with aching joints, sweating, fever and a headache. This can then clear up completely, and the person may carry on for months or years without any problems. In some people, the virus gradually attacks the immune system and can cause full-blown AIDS.

## SYMPTOMS AND EFFECTS OF AIDS

These include losing a lot of weight, very high temperatures, swollen glands and serious infections – including pneumonia (a lung infection), bad gut infections (with diarrhoea) and skin infections. Many people develop tumours, such as skin cancers, all over their body. In many people, AIDS is a fatal disease.

**TESTING FOR HIV**

Anyone who has had sex with someone who might have HIV should get a blood test. People at special risk include those who have several sexual partners, and intravenous drug users. Straight and gay people are all at risk if they have sex with a high-risk partner – someone who has had previous sexual relationships and has not used barrier methods of protection, e.g. condoms.

The important thing to remember about HIV testing is that it can take three or four months between becoming infected and a test showing positive. Therefore, it is important to get some counselling from your doctor or a specialist at a clinic to decide when you should be checked. Some people know they are at risk of HIV but avoid doing anything about it, because they don't want to be embarrassed by having to talk about their sex lives. Because of this, they continue having unsafe sex, become infected if they weren't already, and go on to infect other people. Finding the courage to get advice early could save your own life and many others.

**POSSIBLE TREATMENTS**

There is still no cure for AIDS, although some people have now survived for about twenty years. Most people are treated with a large number of drugs called immuno-suppressants. These attempt to control the virus, preventing further immune problems, but they have unpleasant side-effects, including nausea and diarrhoea, and can make the person vulnerable to other infections.

# 7 Other Illnesses That Can Make Life Miserable

**This chapter covers:**

- ME/Chronic Fatigue Syndrome
- Glandular Fever
- Adolescent Tonsillitis
- Migraine
- Acne

These diseases may not be life-threatening, but they are all fairly common in teenagers and, without the right sort of help and treatment, can be annoying or make life miserable.

## ME/Chronic Fatigue Syndrome

### WHAT IS IT?

ME (myalgic encephalopathy), chronic fatigue syndrome (CFS) or post-viral fatigue syndrome (PVFS) are all names for a condition that affects many thousands of people every year. It can strike at any age but is particularly common in teenagers. While it definitely does exist, it's very hard to say exactly what it is. There is no single test to prove that you do or don't have it, so medical professionals can only recognise it from a particular set of symptoms.

It's possible that these symptoms are actually caused by different illnesses, but they are generally grouped together for recognition and treatment. The illness often starts after a short viral infection, e.g. flu or glandular fever or even a simple cold. Instead of recovering, the ME sufferer starts to develop a whole range of uncomfortable symptoms and weaknesses.

**SYMPTOMS AND EFFECTS**

These include:

- overwhelming and chronic tiredness;
- muscle weakness;
- heavy and/or painful limbs;
- severe lack of concentration;
- very poor short-term memory;
- reduced appetite;
- hypersensitivity to noise and touch.

Not surprisingly with all these symptoms, sufferers often become depressed.

**POSSIBLE TREATMENTS**

Apart from rest, one of the most important factors in recovery is to find a sympathetic doctor or health professional. Because there is no one standard treatment, you may have to try different approaches. Getting over ME takes effort, and having an encouraging and helpful doctor or clinic can make a big difference!

Some doctors consider ME to be a physical illness and others a psychological illness, so they will approach it in different ways. Just to confuse matters even more, some treatments that work very well for one person will be useless for another.

However, the most effective treatments seem to be:

- adequate rest during the initial acute phase of the illness and during any relapse;
- cognitive-behaviour therapy – a special form of talking therapy

that helps you to readjust your feelings about what you can and can't do;

- a *very* carefully graded exercise programme (hydrotherapy in a warm hospital pool is particularly effective) under the supervision of a physiotherapist or other expert (but you have to be extremely careful not to overdo the exercise as this can make the illness worse);
- regular healthy meals;
- trying to get your body clock back in check – many ME sufferers end up sleeping during the day and being restless at night. Be strict with yourself so that even if you're resting or watching TV during daylight hours you still try to make sure that, however tired you may feel, you don't go to sleep until it is dark.

This illness may involve a long time out of school, and it's important that you get home educational support and, when you do go back to school, you do it gradually, e.g. starting off with half-days. Your doctor should be able to write you a letter for the school explaining this. For excellent support and information contact the ME Association (see Contacts).

## Glandular Fever

**WHAT IS IT?**

Glandular fever (or infectious mononucleosis) is an acute viral infection that affects the body's immune system. It is most common in fifteen- to seventeen-year-olds, is spread by coughing and the exchange of saliva, e.g. through kissing, and you're more likely to develop the illness if you come into contact with it when you are particularly tired or run down. A simple blood test diagnoses glandular fever.

## SYMPTOMS AND EFFECTS

Glandular fever usually starts with a high temperature and a sore throat – probably the worst you've ever had in your life – plus:

- swollen glands in the neck and possibly armpits and groin;
- night sweats;
- abdominal pain;
- aching head and limbs.

It can occasionally affect your liver, making you feel particularly grim, and for that reason sufferers are advised not to drink alcohol for a year or so after the infection.

## POSSIBLE TREATMENTS

Most patients recover after six to eight weeks without any drug treatments. As glandular fever is caused by a virus, antibiotics will have no effect. In fact, some antibiotics will cause a rash in glandular fever sufferers. Most people need about a month's rest to help them recover, but you may feel tired and miserable for up to a year afterwards. There is also evidence that someone who has suffered once from glandular fever can have less serious episodes later in life when they become particularly tired and run down.

# Adolescent Tonsillitis

## WHAT IS IT?

Tonsillitis means 'inflammation of the tonsils'. These are little glands at the back of the throat which produce white blood cells to help fight bugs and infections. They're usually the size of a pea, but, when infected, can swell to the size of a large grape and be extremely painful.

Most people have tonsillitis when they are very young, but develop resistance to it by the time they are six or seven. Others seem to have a particular weakness in this part of their body. Like many other illnesses, it's particularly common when someone is run down or burning the candle at both ends.

## SYMPTOMS AND EFFECTS

Tonsillitis often comes on very fast with a severe sore throat and very high temperature. You will feel very unwell indeed.

In severe cases, there is a risk of quinsy, which is an abscess (a big collection of pus) around the tonsils. This can become so large that it stops you being able to swallow anything except saliva and it may need emergency surgical treatment.

## POSSIBLE TREATMENTS

Tonsillitis can be a viral or bacterial infection and, because antibiotics don't work against viruses, doctors often prefer to wait a couple of days to see if the infection clears on its own before prescribing any drugs. In the meantime, painkillers like paracetamol are very useful, particularly if you can use the soluble kind. Gargling with soluble aspirin can help reduce pain and discomfort considerably, but no one under twelve should take aspirin as it can cause serious side-effects in some young people.

You probably won't feel like eating very much, but it's important to drink lots of fluids. If you are prescribed antibiotics, it's easier to take them in liquid form or, if you have been given pills instead of liquid, try swallowing them with something thick like a smoothie or milkshake.

If you keep getting tonsillitis, your doctor may take a swab from the back of your throat to check out which particular bug is causing it. If it happens as often as six times a year, they may recommend that you have your tonsils removed. This is a surgical operation done under a general anaesthetic, and you'll need to stay in hospital at least overnight. It can leave you feeling quite sore and weak for a week or so afterwards, but for sufferers of severe recurrent tonsillitis it is usually worth it.

## Amy's Story

Amy had been getting tonsillitis from ever since she could remember. Whenever a cold went around her primary school she would be off for at least a week, so her mum was used to watching out for the symptoms. Things got a little better when she was nine or ten, but then after she moved up to secondary school it all got worse again.

Amy found that every time she got tired or run down she would also get ill. She had a starring role in the school play but, by the end of the dress rehearsal, had a soaring temperature and hardly any voice, so she couldn't perform.

As her GCSEs approached, Amy missed more and more school, though she took care to catch up with as much of the work as possible. Each attack would start in the same way. She'd feel a bit tired and shaky, lose her appetite and within twelve to twenty-four hours would have a high temperature and severe pain. After three particularly bad bouts of tonsillitis, her doctor took a swab from the back of Amy's throat, which suggested that, on this occasion at least, there was a bacterial infection. After that, Amy's mum kept some antibiotics at home for Amy to take as soon as an attack started.

The low point came in the winter before Amy's GCSEs, when her illness almost lost her one of her best friends, Molly. She and Molly had been close for years, but things became strained when Molly had met and started going out with her first serious boyfriend. Amy felt a bit left out, especially when Molly talked non-stop about the new love in her life. Unfortunately, just when Amy was getting ill with her fourth attack of tonsillitis in six months, Molly started having problems and broke up with her boyfriend. She called Amy for advice and sympathy, but Amy was too ill to talk – and had no voice left anyway. Molly felt let down and started spreading rumours that Amy was attention-seeking and exaggerating how sick she was. When Amy went back to school the following week, things were very difficult and it took a long time before their friendship settled down again.

Her doctor had been talking for some time about an operation to remove her tonsils, so Amy spoke to her mum and decided that she would like to go ahead in the summer after her exams. The GP made an appointment for Amy to see an ear, nose and throat (ENT) consultant, who agreed that she would benefit from the operation and also felt that the summer would be a good time to give her time to recuperate from the surgery. Everything went well, and although Amy's throat was very uncomfortable for about ten days after the operation it was nothing like as painful as her worst bout of tonsillitis. By the time she went back to school in September, she realised that she felt better than she had done for years and, that winter, she had hardly any time off sick at all.

# Migraine

**WHAT IS IT?**

A severe headache, sometimes affecting only one side of the head, which can last from two hours to two days.

About one in ten people suffers from migraine and they usually have their first attack before the age of twenty. There's no single cause, but migraine tends to run in families. Each sufferer will have their own triggers – things which tend to set off an attack. These triggers can include:

- stress or emotional excitement;
- changes of routine and climate;
- particular foods, e.g. chocolate, cheese, red wine, citrus fruit;
- flickering or bright lights;
- loud noises.

Women are more likely to have migraines around the time of their period, and taking the contraceptive pill can sometimes make them worse.

**SYMPTOMS AND EFFECTS**
These include:

- severe headache, usually at the front and often only one side of the head. The pain may come on gradually, often accompanied by stomach ache, nausea or vomiting;
- visual disturbance – shimmering or zigzags in front of the eyes;
- dislike of bright light. Once the pain has achieved full force, most people just want; to lie down in the dark, because any light or movement makes them worse.

Migraine often occurs at times of major stress, but for some people it happens when the normal pressures of life lift a little, e.g. at weekends or on holiday.

Because the symptoms of migraine are fairly typical, special tests are rarely necessary for diagnosis. However, if the headache is changing or you get tingling in your limbs or other symptoms associated with the migraine, your doctor may want to refer you for scans or neurological tests, just to rule out any other problems.

**POSSIBLE TREATMENTS**

Painkillers can help, but if you're feeling very nauseous they can be difficult to keep down. Special migraine pills are available at pharmacies. These include an anti-nausea drug, which will make you feel a bit better. However, if you suffer from recurrent migraine you should see your family doctor, who can prescribe more effective treatment and even some special drugs that you can take to try to prevent attacks starting in the first place.

One of the most useful things you can do for yourself is to work out what triggers your migraine. Keeping a food and mood diary for a few weeks can help a lot, as you can then see what you've eaten or what has happened to you just before the attacks occur.

# Acne

### WHAT IS IT?

Everyone (particularly teenagers) gets the occasional spot. But acne is severe, recurring spots caused by inflammation of the hair follicles and the tiny sebaceous glands on the skin. These produce an oily substance, called sebum, which 'waterproofs' your skin. During puberty, you tend to produce more sebum, so your skin may look and feel greasy. The pores can become blocked with the oily sebum and the normal bacteria that everyone has on their skin gets behind this, causing infected swellings, i.e. spots. Severe acne is a common cause of depression in teenagers.

### SYMPTOMS AND EFFECTS

Acne usually occurs on the face, but also often affects the neck, back, shoulders and chest. It shows up as:

- crops of spots at different stages;
- some very red and inflamed spots with yellow centres of pus.

Most people grow out of acne after a few years, but it can still cause a lot of anguish in the meantime. Luckily, doctors are sympathetic to this and understand how upsetting it can be. They are also sensitive to the fact that people suffering from acne may often be called names or bullied.

**POSSIBLE TREATMENTS**

No matter what you may hear, acne is not caused by eating too many sweets or greasy foods – although they don't do you much good either! It can be difficult to get rid of, so you have to treat it quite aggressively. Try to do the following:

- Keep your skin as clean as possible by using a medicated soap or lotion from a supermarket or pharmacy.
- Use spot cream to help dry the spots out.
- Get some fresh air (and sunshine if possible) every day, as this also helps dry out the skin.
- Talk to the pharmacist at the prescription counter if these suggestions don't work, as they can sell you stronger creams and lotions that are not on obvious display.
- If these haven't worked after three or four weeks, go and talk to your GP. He/she can prescribe special ointments or pills to zap the acne – though you'll have to use them for at least four weeks before you see a real difference. Sometimes even this isn't enough and your doctor may arrange for you to see a dermatologist (a doctor specialising in skin) for more treatment.
- Everyone is tempted to squeeze their spots – but there's a risk of transferring germs from dirty fingernails and pushing the

infection deeper down into your skin, causing a worse problem. If you must squeeze, make sure your hands and nails are really clean and then cover your fingers in a clean tissue.

## Sam's Story

Sam started getting his first bad spots at fourteen, just about the time when he suddenly grew around eight centimetres in height. At first they were on his face, but within a few months they were all over his upper chest and back. He took to wearing a white T-shirt under his school shirt so that no one would see them when he got changed for sport — and was so successful in hiding them that not even his mum realised how bad the problem was.

She did, however, notice that he had some particularly nasty spots on his face and 'tactfully' left him some cleansing lotion and spot gel in his bedroom. He tried using these, and they helped for a bit, but he still kept getting breakthroughs of acne. He made a couple of trips to the chemist himself and bought what seemed to be stronger acne treatments, but still nothing did the trick.

Things got a bit better in the summer when sunshine seemed to clear up the spots on Sam's face, but because his upper body was never exposed to sunlight the spots there carried on getting worse. His mum told him not to worry and even offered him some concealer make-up to hide the worst spots, but he wouldn't risk anyone noticing it and making fun of him at school. As it was, some of his friends already made jokes about his acne, and Sam was really worried that it would mean he'd never be able to find a girlfriend.

Things came — literally — to a head when one particularly nasty spot on the bridge of his nose became infected. Of course, Sam knew you shouldn't squeeze spots, but sometimes you just have to, don't you? This time it got worse and worse until it was enormous and bright red and felt as though it was throbbing like a warning light. He felt so self-conscious that he brushed his hair forward and kept trying to hold his hand in front of his face, but his mum noticed, insisted on having a look and then said he had to see the doctor. She made an appointment and went with him to make sure he went in. Much to Sam's surprise, the GP was very helpful and didn't tell him off for squeezing the spot. She asked if there were problems anywhere else, and Sam reluctantly removed his T-shirt so his doctor could have a look at the full extent of the acne. He left the surgery with a prescription for six weeks of antibiotic tablets and some antibiotic cream. The doctor told him that it would take a few weeks before he noticed any difference, but in about two weeks things were already starting to improve. After six weeks his skin was almost totally clear, although there were still marks where the worst spots had been. Sam continued taking antibiotics for four months in total and then found that when he stopped, so had the spots. He still gets the odd one now and then, but finds that he can keep his acne under control by using his acne lotion from the chemist and his antibiotic cream if a spot looks like becoming infected.

# 8 How to Stay Healthy

**This chapter covers:**

- Exercise
- Tips on Getting Active
- Diet and Health
- Health Consequences of Smoking
- Good Sexual Health
- Positive Mental Health

It may seem hard to believe, but it really is true that what you do as a child and a young person has a big effect on how healthy you are likely to be as an adult and on how long you will live. Some things that you either do, or fail to do, won't kill you in the next hours or days but may shorten your life eventually. This chapter looks at the main things that can affect your health in the long term – these are the amount of exercise you do, your diet and whether you smoke. Smoking causes the highest number of avoidable deaths, followed by being obese (very overweight) and not taking enough exercise. All these risk factors increase the chances of someone getting heart disease as well as many other serious health problems. Many of these issues are interrelated – people who smoke are often the same people who also overeat, take no exercise and generally don't take care of themselves. This chapter also looks at how to avoid sexually transmitted diseases and unplanned pregnancy, and how to take care of your mental and emotional health.

## Exercise

Lack of exercise affects more than your looks! Couch potatoes are also damaging their heart. Failing to take any exercise adds to the risk of heart disease as much as smoking a packet of cigarettes every day. And heart disease is the most common cause of premature death (death under the age of seventy-five) in the UK.

**FACT**

About a quarter of premature deaths in men and around seventeen per cent in women are caused by heart disease.

So – lack of exercise can kill you.

If you take no physical exercise this will double your chances of developing heart disease and also increase the chances of you suffering other diseases such as diabetes. Even moderate exercise, such as a brisk walk for thirty minutes most days, will help to control weight, cut stress and help reduce anxiety and depression.

### Effects of Exercise on Mental and Emotional Well-Being

A survey by the mental health charity MIND has shown that most people with mental health problems find that exercise helps lift their mood or fight stress. Two-thirds of people in the study found that exercise helped with the symptoms of depression, and about half felt it helped with stress or anxiety. Most said that it helped them improve their motivation, so they generally felt better about life.

The bad news is that doctors estimate between sixty-five and eighty-five per cent of the world's population fail to take enough exercise.

And the really bad news is that the old are fitter than the young! A survey carried out for the BBC showed that, on an average day, Britons aged between eight and nineteen years spent one hour and fifteen minutes doing any form of physical activity, compared with the over-sixty-fives, who spent one hour and forty minutes.

Though teenage boys are more active than girls, after the age of twenty women tend to take more exercise than men.

One thing that really worries doctors is that the amount of physical exercise you do as a child and teenager influences how active you are likely to be in later life. In other words, many people who exercise a lot as young people go on to exercise all their life, while those who never get up off the sofa in childhood are unlikely to take up exercise when they are middle-aged.

The British Heart Foundation has pointed out that although the rate of people dying early from heart disease is falling at the moment, it's very likely to increase again unless today's children and young people become more active.

Another brilliant effect of exercise is that it strengthens your bones and joints and makes it less likely that you will suffer from osteoporosis (weakened bones, which often fracture) in later life.

## *Recommended Levels of Exercise for Children and Young People*

Most doctors and exercise specialists agree that between the ages of five and eighteen children and young people should spend at least one hour each day doing moderately intense activity. This could include:

- cycling;
- running;
- dancing;
- competitive team games, such as football, hockey or netball.

## *Tips on Getting Active*

- If you haven't done any exercise for years it is important to build up the sessions gradually. And choosing an activity you enjoy means you are more likely to go on doing it. Try simple things like walking instead of taking the bus or tube.
- During exercise, your pulse rate should increase and you should feel a bit out of breath. At the end you should feel a bit tired and your muscles should ache a little. It's not necessary to exercise so hard that you're completely exhausted!
- Don't forget to drink plenty of water as you're exercising, especially if the outside temperature is warm. Getting even five per cent dehydrated will cause your performance to suffer a lot. A good test to see if you're drinking enough is to look at the colour of the urine you produce when you go to the toilet after an exercise session. It should be pale yellow. If it is a darker orange or brown, this is a sign that you need to drink more.
- Some people find that drinking tap water is fine while others feel that special 'sports' drinks give them more energy and help them to recover faster. It is really a matter of personal preference – and how much you want to spend.

- Whatever exercise you choose, it is important to keep safe. So if you are taking up running, for example, always go with a friend, stick to well-lit places and make sure you can be seen easily – especially if you are out as it gets dark. Never be tempted to listen to music as you run – it will stop you from hearing the traffic noises and could make you a target for attack.

EXERCISE DOESN'T HAVE TO BE BORING!

## Diet and Health

### What Makes a Good Diet?

The key to a good diet is . . . balance!

Eating a variety of different food types in the right kind of quantities allows your body to stay healthy – now and in the future.

During puberty – roughly between the ages of nine and sixteen – your body grows very fast. This means that you need more energy from your food than an adult does. You probably already know that the energy in your diet is measured in terms of 'kilocalories', or 'calories' for short. If you add up the number of calories in your diet and then add up how many you use to exercise, to grow and to keep all your normal body processes going, these numbers should be roughly equal. If you take in more calories than you need, you will get fat. If you use up more than you take in, you will lose weight. Simple!

### What Should Teenagers Eat?

A healthy diet is like a pyramid. At the bottom you have all the foods that you should be eating most of. These include carbohydrates, such as rice, pasta, breakfast cereals, potatoes and bread as well as at least five portions of fruit and vegetables every day. You should have a portion of carbohydrates at each meal. 'Average' portions include two large slices of bread, a 200-gramme potato or 100 grammes of (cooked) rice or pasta.

The middle of the pyramid is made up of foods that contain more protein, e.g. meat, fish, eggs, or – for vegetarians – pulses and beans, and dairy products (milk, cheese and yoghurt – equivalent to a pint of milk a day).

At the very top are the foods you probably already know aren't very good for you! These are the combined sugary and fatty foods such as doughnuts, cakes and biscuits, and other high-fat foods such as chips, crisps and over-processed fast food.

## What Is Wrong With Sugary Foods?

When we eat foods containing sugar, the body produces a hormone called insulin, which helps to move the sugar from the bloodstream into the liver, where it can be stored as a source of energy for later. If we eat a large amount of sugar quickly (e.g. in the form of sweets or chocolate), the body often produces too much insulin, and the effect is to clear the sugar from the blood too quickly. This can cause a feeling of dizziness and nausea – and also a craving for more sugar. If this happens, people often find themselves eating more and more sugar – they seem to need a sugar 'fix'. It is also thought that this is one of the reasons why there are more and more people developing diabetes – because the pancreas gland has become exhausted and cannot carry on producing enough insulin. So it is much better to eat foods that contain the type of sugar that is more difficult to digest and therefore that goes into the bloodstream more slowly. These include bananas, wholemeal bread and cereals – especially porridge oats.

## What Is Wrong With High-Fat Foods?

High-fat foods are 'calorie dense' – this means that for a certain weight of food they have a high number of calories, and therefore can make you get fat quite easily. They can also make the level of fats in the blood increase and cause damage to the blood vessels and the heart. So, again, they should be eaten in moderation.

### Should Boys and Girls Eat the Same Amounts?

The sexes may be equal in most ways, but boys do need to eat more during their growth spurts than girls. Girls tend to start growing at around the age of ten. This is one of the first signs of puberty in girls, and it usually means that their periods will start about two years later. Boys have their main growth spurt later on in puberty, usually at around twelve. This is why many girls are taller than the boys in Years Seven and Eight. The boys catch up soon afterwards and often go on to be taller and heavier.

In the growth spurt, boys and girls grow between about twenty to twenty-five centimetres in height and they gain about twenty to twenty-six kilogrammes in weight. In boys, most of this weight is in the form of extra muscle as they get taller and stronger. But girls develop softer, more curved figures during puberty, so a lot of their extra weight goes on as fat around their bust and hips. Some girls become very upset at this change in their bodies, and it can be one of the triggers for developing an eating disorder. It is important to realise that women's bodies are *meant* to look different, and this new distribution of fat is normal.

### Important Nutrients

A good balanced diet with lots of fresh fruit and vegetables should supply all the nutrients you need. But some are particularly important in helping you grow and keeping you healthy.

#### CALCIUM

Recent studies have suggested that about one in four girls don't have enough calcium in their diet. This can affect the strength of their bones, resulting in broken bones later in life. For healthy bone development and growth, teenagers need about eight hundred to one thousand milligrammes of calcium per day plus some vitamin D and phosphorous.

#### SOURCES OF CALCIUM

1 pint of full cream milk = 660 milligrammes
1 pint of semi-skimmed milk = 690 milligrammes
28 grammes of hard cheese = 190 milligrammes
3 slices of brown or white bread = 100 milligrammes

So one pint of milk and a piece of cheese on toast could provide just about enough calcium for one day.

## IRON

Iron is needed to make red blood cells, which carry oxygen around the body. If someone doesn't have enough iron in their diet, their body manages for a while by using up its reserve stock. After this they may become anaemic, which can make them feel tired and breathless.

Girls need plenty of iron to make up for the blood they lose when they have a period. Studies have shown that about one in six teenage girls has low iron stores, so they can easily become anaemic.

Iron is found mainly in red meat, but other good sources are breakfast cereals (look at the small print on the side of the box – you'll be amazed at what is added!) and green leafy vegetables. Some people think spinach is a good source of iron – it does have iron in it, but only the same amount as other leafy vegetables. When the calculations about its content were first done, some-one got them wrong and for a long time people thought that spinach had ten times more iron in it than it actually has.

Vitamin C helps you to absorb iron more efficiently, so drink-ing fresh orange juice or any other drink rich in vitamin C will help you absorb more of the iron in the food you eat at the same time. On the other hand, caffeinated drinks like tea will reduce the amount of iron that is absorbed.

## Water

Water is not a nutrient – it doesn't contain any calories or vitamins, etc., but it is an important part of our diet. About fifty to seventy per cent of your body weight is made up of water, and if you didn't drink any fluids at all, you could only survive for a few days. Water is vital for lots of metabolic processes in the body, and a lack of it – or other fluids containing water – can make you dehydrated.

**EFFECTS OF DEHYDRATION ON THE BODY**

| Short-term | Long-term |
| --- | --- |
| Headaches | Kidney stones |
| Tiredness | Urine infections |
| Poor concentration | Constipation |
| Bad breath | |
| Nausea | |

**HOW MUCH IS ENOUGH WATER?**

An average adult should drink two and a half litres of water a day. That's about ten average glasses of water! Some of this can actually be obtained from the water that is present in other items of your diet, e.g. soups, fruit, yoghurt, etc. But most people should be drinking at least six glasses of water per day.

If it is hot or if you exercise – and especially if you sweat – then you need to increase this amount. The best way of drinking water is plain old tap water. Fruit juice contains about ninety per cent water, so it is not as refreshing as plain water. There are no real advantages to drinking bottled water. Some brands have added minerals or gas, but there's no good evidence that they are any better for your health, although, of course, you may prefer the taste.

**FIZZY DRINKS**

Young people who drink 'regular' (i.e. not low-calorie) fizzy drinks are much more likely to be overweight than those who drink milk or water. Most sweet fizzy drinks contain nothing but sugar and flavouring, so they are a source of 'empty' calories and rot your teeth. The best advice is to stop drinking them altogether. The 'diet' or low-calorie versions are much less harmful, but there are still some concerns about the possible effects they could have because, for example, of their high caffeine content.

## Is it True That Children and Young People Are Getting Fatter?

A recent study of primary school children in Leeds showed that one in six children was obese – severely overweight. The researchers said they were really worried about what the effects of this would be on the children's hearts and joints. The children were weighed and measured each year for six years, and during this time more and more children were found to be overweight – so the problem seems to be getting worse very quickly. Although the young people in the study were taller at the end of the six years than the researchers would have predicted from measuring their heights at the beginning, they had gained even more weight than they would have expected, so they had definitely got fatter. The reason this happened was thought to be a combination of two things: the children were doing less exercise and they were eating more unhealthy food.

## How Can I Find Out What I Should Weigh?

Children or young people of the same age may be very different heights and weights and you can only tell if they are a healthy weight for their height by plotting the measurements on a growth chart.

Your height will be affected by your parents' heights as well as by what you eat. And children who are ill while they are still growing often end up shorter than they would have been if they were well.

If you want to check your own height and weight to see if you have anything to worry about, ask your school nurse or family doctor to measure you accurately and get them to plot the measurements on a chart.

## How Can I Lose Weight?

If you are still growing (and most people carry on growing until the age of about seventeen), you may simply have to try to keep your weight the same while your height goes up – that way you will automatically look slimmer as you grow. If you have stopped growing, you might decide that it would be healthier to lose a little bit of weight.

#### GOLDEN RULES FOR DIETING

- Don't try any very restrictive diets – you need foods from each of the food groups mentioned above, and if you cut out any groups you may end up with a diet that is too low in certain vitamins or minerals.
- Reduce the amount of sugary and fatty food you eat.
- Do try to increase the amount of exercise you do – but, again, don't do too much too soon.
- Don't try to lose weight too fast – a healthy weight loss is no more than half a kilogramme each week.
- Don't carry on dieting once you have reached a healthy weight for your height. Being too thin can be as bad for your health as being too fat.

## *What Is so Bad About Being Fat?*

If you are overweight as a child, you are much more likely to be overweight as an adult. This can lead to lots of serious health problems:

- The fattest group of men in the population have three times the risk of dying in any particular year compared with men who are a normal weight for their height.
- Obesity and lack of exercise are thought to account for one in three cases of cancer of the colon (bowel), stomach, breast and kidney.
- In adults, premature deaths related to obesity are now second only to deaths due to smoking.

# Health Consequences of Smoking

Some of the bad news about smoking was covered in Chapter 6. In this section we look at more of the health consequences of smoking. We know that the earlier someone starts smoking the greater the risk that they will be a lifetime smoker – the best advice is never to start.

## *Risks*

- People who smoke are much more likely than non-smokers to get lung diseases. These include asthma, chest infections and, in the long term, unpleasant diseases like emphysema (where the divisions between segments of the lung collapse and people get very breathless) and lung cancer. Lung cancer is a particularly nasty form of cancer. It is often found in smokers in their forties or fifties. It is difficult to treat, as it often spreads to areas such as the brain and bones before it is diagnosed.

- Many people don't realise how bad smoking is for the heart and blood vessels. Smoking is thought to cause thousands of heart attacks each year, and about two thousand people end up having to have a leg amputated because of the effect of smoking on the arteries that supply the leg with blood.
- It is thought that about one hundred and twenty thousand people in the UK die prematurely (sooner than they should have died) every year because they smoke.
- Other effects of smoking include: bad breath, dry and wrinkly skin, smelly hair and clothes, stained teeth and fingers, and looking older than you are.
- Smoking is a really expensive habit – and many young people end up not eating properly in order to afford to smoke.

## Good Sexual Health

You may have seen some of the newspaper headlines in the last few years – such as: *Teen Infection Rates Double in Ten Years* and *Sexual Health of UK Adolescents Very Poor*. There is no doubt that the number of sexually transmitted infections (STIs) that are diagnosed has increased. This, some believe, is partly because people are less embarrassed than they used to be about going to see a doctor about a possible infection. Also, more young people are now tested for specific infections, so more cases are being found.

However, the increase is still worrying, and two infections that are increasing rapidly among young people are chlamydia and genital warts. If infections are not treated quickly, they can have permanent effects on health and fertility. In the UK in 2001, more than 1.3 million new sexually transmitted infections were diagnosed in the specialist genito-urinary medicine (GUM or 'Special') clinics, and most of these were in young women under the age of twenty.

You may not be sexually active yet, but whether you are or not, it is important to know that if you want to be sure to protect yourself from the possibility of a sexually transmitted infection or pregnancy, you need to practise safe sex. This means taking precautions to avoid infection (by using a condom) as well as precautions to avoid pregnancy (in young people the pill is the most effective form of contraception).

## Chlamydia

A bug called *Chlamydia trachomatis* causes the infection called chlamydia. It affects both sexes, but causes most long-term harm to girls and women. It is passed on very easily between people who have unprotected sex. It is the most common STI caused by a bacterium. The really worrying thing about chlamydia is that it doesn't cause any symptoms or signs in about half the men and most of the women who have it, so people are not even aware that they are infected and can therefore spread the infection to others during unprotected sex.

The most common symptoms in women who do notice anything wrong are an increase in vaginal discharge, some pain on passing urine and having to go to the toilet to pass urine more often, and mild stomach ache. Men can have a whitish discharge from the penis, and they may get pain when they pass urine.

Chlamydia is usually easy to treat with antibiotics, but if the problem is not diagnosed and treated it can lead to infertility in both men and women.

## Genital Warts

You may have had warts on your fingers or verrucas on your feet. These are different types of warts, caused by strains of the same wart 'family'. Genital warts (which can occur anywhere on the genital area in men and women) are caused by a virus called the human papilloma virus (HPV). This is a sexually transmitted infection spread by close contact – which could mean just touching rather than penetrative sex.

The warts often appear in clusters. They are small lumps, which are usually flat and pinkish-brown. Sometimes they can spread a lot and look like tiny cauliflowers. They are usually painless. They are the most frequent sexually transmitted infection seen in GUM clinics. Lots of people are thought to have the wart virus in their body, but it only becomes active in some people.

The warts can be treated with a special liquid, which is painted on to the surface. The big worry about catching warts is that in women they are associated with the risk of getting cervical cancer. This is cancer of the neck of the womb and is the most common cancer affecting women under the age of thirty-five.

The risk of developing cervical cancer is also increased in smokers, people who have lots of sexual partners (because of the increased chance of catching warts) and people who start having sex when they are very young, when the tissues are more delicate and infection is more likely to take hold.

## *Pregnancy*

You are likely to have noticed headlines such as: *UK Heads Teen Pregnancy Rates*. You probably know that if girls get pregnant in their early teenage years, they are likely to miss out on education and they and their babies are not usually as healthy as those born to older mothers. What you may not know is that, after admissions to hospital following accidents, the next most common reason for a teenager to be in hospital is for a termination of pregnancy (abortion) or to deliver a baby. There is a lot of work going on at the moment to help young people to make good choices about whether they want to be sexually active or not. This includes encouraging them to put off having sex until they are older as well as making sure they have good access to contraception and sexual health advice if they need it.

# Positive Mental Health

It's easy to think of health as being purely physical, but it's important to take care of your mental and emotional health as well.

### *What Is Good Mental Health?*

Just as a balanced diet is vital for good nutrition, so a balanced range of relationships and interests can help protect you from the stresses and pressures that contribute to mental health problems. If you think about how you spend your time and your energy, you'll probably find it divides into roughly five groups:

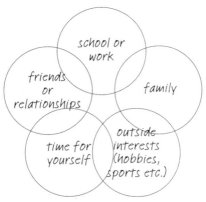

Of course, it would be silly to pretend that these areas remain equal in size and importance all the time. They are constantly changing.

Whenever there are exams coming up at school, I feel really stressed out. There's so much revision and coursework, and my parents want me to do well. It feels as though it's taking over my life and there's no time left for anything else at all.

*Dan, 16*

I've been bullied for nearly a year and I dread going to school now. Even weekends and holidays are ruined, because I'm just so worried about going back. I don't have any friends, so there's nowhere to go out of school anyway.

*Sam, 14*

I don't know why, but my mum and I are at each other's throats the whole time. I can feel the atmosphere as soon as I walk into the house, so I try to avoid her as much as possible. Of course this makes her even more angry, and the rows start up again.

*Katie, 17*

However, research shows us that people who lead a balanced emotional life are likely to be better able to face problems and challenges, resolving and learning from them. They'll also be more confident, more flexible and sympathetic to others, better able to enjoy themselves and generally be more popular – and successful.

## *Why Do Things Go Wrong?*

Mental health problems cover anything from feeling a bit anxious and low over a fallout with a friend to severe depression and psychiatric illness. One in four people suffers a mental health problem every year, although, of course, most of them get through it, either because the problem solves itself or they get the help they need. Sadly, too few people – and particularly too few young people – are prepared to ask for help with these kinds of problems, and this can result in situations spiralling out of control.

For example, many people who are addicted to alcohol or drugs started using them as a form of self-medication. They may have been anxious or depressed or trying to cope with something they couldn't see an answer to, and getting drunk or high gave them a short-term escape. Unfortunately, the 'treatment' becomes as bad as or worse than the original problem.

There are also various risk factors in family life that can increase the likelihood of young people suffering mental health problems. These include:

- poverty;
- poor housing;
- parental rows and separation or divorce;
- physical, sexual or emotional abuse;
- bereavement;
- a family member with a psychiatric illness, including depression;
- a family member with an alcohol or drug problem.

### How Can You Protect Your Mental Health?

Look again at the diagram on page 171. How much time and effort do you spend on each area? Which areas make you happiest? And which cause you most grief? Consider asking for help from a friend, adult or helpline to sort out anything you aren't happy with. For more suggestions, see Chapter 10 and the Contacts section.

Other suggestions include:

- Make time to do things that you enjoy, and give yourself rewards for time spent on revision or chores.
- Be proactive rather than reactive all the time. If you think nothing exciting ever happens in your life, then it's time to start making plans for yourself rather than rely on others to do it for you.

- Cherish your friends but don't be scared to go out and make new ones. Being comfortable meeting new people (even if you never see them again) is an important part of acquiring self-confidence and will pay dividends when it comes to further education or getting a job.
- Try listening to other people's points of view, even if you don't agree with them.
- Make sure you get some physical exercise, preferably in the fresh air. It doesn't have to be an organised sport – cycling to school or walking the dog will do just as well. Apart from helping your physical health, the chemicals called endorphins that are released during exercise give you a natural high, so you feel better all round.
- Learn to like yourself. Most of us are our own worst critics. Instead of thinking about all the things you can't do or you don't like about yourself, make a list of your positive attributes. Ask a close friend or one of your family to help you. You could be surprised at the things that other people appreciate about you!
- Be prepared to ask for help if you need it.

## Sacha's Story

I've always been quite short – all my family are – but it became really obvious when I was twelve or thirteen and everyone at school was much, much taller than me. I was also late developing and I began to hate games, because the others laughed at me when I was getting changed. I quite like sport, but nobody ever seemed to want me on their team, and I can't blame them, because I wasn't any good at anything. By the time I was nearly fifteen I'd become really introverted. I worked hard at school, but didn't have many close friends and just tended to hang around at home and watch telly in my spare time. I know my mum was worried about me and kept saying she wished

I had more friends and wanted me to go out and do things, but there just didn't seem to be the opportunities. Then I read in the local paper about a circus workshop that was held in town on Saturday mornings. I was interested, but didn't think it would be for me, because I didn't have any circus skills and I wasn't talented in anything like that. But my mum encouraged me to give it a go and all it said in the paper was that anyone interested should turn up at this hall at ten a.m. I went along and hung around outside for ages. I saw a few people go in, but they all had kit with them and seemed to know each other. I'd even decided to give up and go back home and I started walking down the road, but I suddenly thought how cross I'd be with myself if I didn't at least try, so I went back and put my head around the door. There were about fifteen people there, some younger, some older than me, but they were really friendly. The guy in charge saw me, drew me in and introduced me to another girl who had come for the first time. He started us off on some juggling, but encouraged everyone else to show us what they were doing as well.

We had a great time, and I've been going ever since. I've met lots of new people, and I've taken part in shows and carnivals, something the old shy me would never have dreamed of. I didn't say anything about it at school at first, but gradually they got to know about it and somehow it seems I'm more popular there as well. I'm very glad I didn't give up and take the bus home that day.

Sacha, 17

## Carrie's Story

I've had epilepsy ever since I was a baby, and I have to take drugs every day to make sure I don't have a fit. Even then I still do sometimes have the odd fit, and because of this my mum and dad are very protective. In fact, they're too protective! As a result I don't have much life outside home or school, although I do have some good friends. We spend a lot of time on the phone together, but I know they also go out and do stuff that I probably wouldn't be able to do. Or wouldn't be allowed to! When I was fourteen a couple of my friends started having boyfriends. Nothing very serious, but it was all they talked about, and they had even less time for me. I felt really left out. Then I had a while off school when I was ill and had to have some more tests done, and when I went back I felt I didn't really belong. I started making excuses not to go to school and for a bit my mum was quite easy-going. And then she got worried about the whole exam thing and took me to see our doctor, who said she'd like me to have a word with a counsellor who works at the practice. Although I didn't like the idea, I went along. The weird thing was although I didn't know what I was going to say it just seemed to pour out once I'd started. I told the counsellor how unhappy and different and lonely I felt at school and how much I wanted to be like other girls. She listened and listened and then, after a couple of sessions, suggested that we try to agree a list of targets. Part of it was about me going to school, but she also encouraged me to talk to my mum about giving me more freedom. And she suggested that I speak to one of my best friends about my feelings. I was a bit worried about this and almost dodged it by sending my friend a jokey e-mail, sort of hoping she'd ignore it. But she came round that evening and honestly seemed to want to know what was happening. When I told her my feelings, her reaction was amazing. She said that they were all worried about me but thought that I didn't want to spend any time with them any more. And she said that she particularly missed me, because I'd always been such a good listener and was the one person she could talk to when she was feeling down who would understand and would help her get her head back together. She was shocked to know how unhappy I was, but somehow it felt good to know how much she appreciated me. From then on, things started to get better.

*Carrie, 16*

# 9 Emergency Tool Kit – Coping With Illnesses and Emergencies

**This chapter covers:**

- Emergency Situations
- Common Symptoms – What to Do and When to Get Help
- The 'Better-Than-Anything-You-Could-Ever-Buy-Ready-Made' First-Aid Kit
- Personal Safety
- Foreign Travel

An important part of growing up is learning to be independent and managing on your own. Sometimes this turns into a real battle – particularly when parents are over-protective or can't believe that you really would be able to cope if anything went wrong. Talking about risks with your family can show you've thought about any dangers and have sensible and practical ideas about how to cope if the worst happens. This can go a long way towards persuading your parents to give you a bit of extra freedom! Whether you're looking forward to spend-ing a night alone in front of the telly while your parents are out partying, a weekend in a caravan in Cornwall with your mates, or planning a trek up Kilimanjaro, the following infor-mation will provide a useful emergency tool kit for most eventualities.

# Emergency Situations

If you are in any doubt about how to cope with an accident or illness then **always get help**. This may mean calling the emergency services (by dialling 999) or stopping a passer-by and asking them to get help for you. Getting help immediately can make the difference between life and death. In these situations, seconds count!

If you go on a resuscitation course, you will learn the basics about how to keep someone alive until help arrives, e.g. from a doctor or an ambulance crew. Some schools and colleges already provide this training, and many young people do a course as part of the Duke of Edinburgh's Award scheme or as part of their swimming and life-saving award training. If these courses are not on offer through school, you could contact St John Ambulance or the British Red Cross, or talk to the person responsible for training in your local hospital.

**SAFETY FIRST**

Never, ever put yourself in danger in order to try to save someone else.

If, for example, you come across a road accident, the best thing to do first is warn other drivers to slow down and stop.

## *Unconsciousness*

Someone may become unconscious as a result of an accident, e.g. a blow to the head or because of a serious medical problem such as a diabetic coma or an overdose of drugs. If you think they are unconscious, check quickly by squeezing them firmly on the shoulder and shouting: 'Are you OK?' Do not shake them or attempt to move their head in case they are suffering from a neck or back injury. If there is no response, then get help immediately.

Shout for help as loudly as you can or ask a passer-by to call the emergency services on 999.

If you have knowledge of first aid, you can check the victim's airway, breathing and circulation. If these are all fine and you are sure they have not suffered a spinal injury, put them in the recovery position to stop them choking on their tongue or vomit if they are sick. This means lying the person on their side, with the head to one side and their uppermost arm and leg stretched out to stop them rolling on their face. This angles their head so that their tongue can fall forward in their mouth rather than backward, blocking the airway, and it allows any vomit or saliva to dribble out rather than choke them.

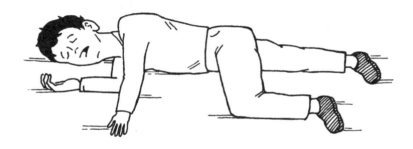

If the person does not seem to be breathing and is not moving or responding to you in any way, then this is very serious. If you know how to resuscitate them, you may save their life.

**Remember:** A is for airway, B is for breathing, C is for circulation.

### A IS FOR AIRWAY

Air needs to get into the lungs through the trachea – a tube that runs down from the back of the throat. If someone is lying on their back and they are unconscious, then this airway can get blocked – because the tongue may flop back and cover the opening. Don't even think about fishing in their mouth for their tongue, because you could push the tongue further back and block the airway. Just tip the person's head back and lift their chin forward. This should open the airway and allow air to go through the trachea into the lungs.

LIFT CHIN
UP AND
FORWARD

**B IS FOR BREATHING**

Look to see if the person's chest is moving up and down – this shows that air is going into the lungs. Bend down and listen over their mouth – can you hear any air as it is breathed out?

If there is no movement or sound, you should give the patient two 'recovery' breaths. This is how you do it:

1. Kneel down next to the patient.
2. Pinch their nose shut to stop air escaping.
3. Take a deep breath in, then bend down and seal your lips over theirs and breathe out into their mouth.
4. At the same time, check to see that their chest moves up.
5. Repeat steps 2 to 4 once more.

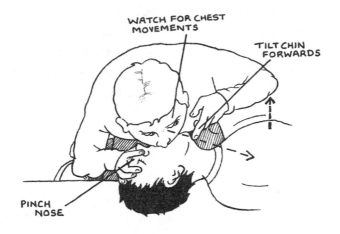

WATCH FOR CHEST MOVEMENTS

TILT CHIN FORWARDS

PINCH NOSE

**C IS FOR CIRCULATION**

If someone's heart stops beating, they will die within a few minutes. The heart pumps blood around the body, and a lack of blood to the brain causes unconsciousness. You can check if someone's heart is beating by feeling for a heartbeat over the left side of their chest – but it can be quite hard to detect, especially if the patient is dressed. If is usually easier to feel for the carotid pulse. This is a strong pulse that can be felt under the chin and

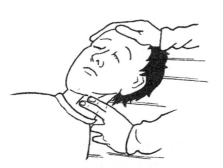

towards the side of the neck – you could practise trying to find it on yourself or a friend.

If you are certain you can't feel a pulse, you should start the 'resuscitation cycle'.

This means doing two things – pressing regularly on their chest to squeeze blood out of the heart and around the body, and providing a supply of air (containing oxygen) from your mouth to theirs.

The place to press is the centre of the chest, over the bottom part of the breastbone where the ribs meet. Put one of your hands over the top of the other, and press through the 'heels' of your hands.

PLACE YOUR HANDS AT THE CENTRE OF THE CHEST OVER THE BOTTOM PART OF THE BREASTBONE

1. First give fifteen chest thrusts at a steady rate. Say to yourself 'one and two and three and...', so you press down every time you say a number and so do just over one compression every second.
2. Then give two breaths of your own air into the person's lungs, as described above.
3. Keep this up until help arrives or until your patient starts breathing for themselves.

## DOC BOX

Anyone who becomes unconscious even for a short period of time as a result of an accident or a blow to the head should be seen by a doctor as soon as possible to rule out injury to the skull or brain. Do not give them anything to eat or drink in the meantime.

## *Choking*

Seeing someone who is choking can be a very scary experience. As above, it is important to try to organise further help by dialling 999 or getting someone else to dial 999 before you start to try to help them yourself. It is important to try not to panic. Common causes of choking include hard sweets and chunks of apple – but people can choke on a variety of foods. Often, they start to laugh while they are eating something, take a breath in and the food goes into the 'wrong' tube at the back of the throat. Instead of travelling down the oesophagus to the stomach, the food goes into the trachea, or windpipe, and gets stuck.

This means that less air can get into the lungs. If the trachea becomes completely blocked, there will be no air supply at all, and the person will become blue and then unconscious.

This is an emergency – the person needs help to get rid of the obstruction as quickly as possible. The first thing to do if the person is still breathing is to encourage them to cough – this may dislodge the object. If this doesn't work, you need to try some blows to the back. To do this you have to stand just to the side and behind the person. Get them to lean slightly forward – you will have to support their chest with one of your hands.

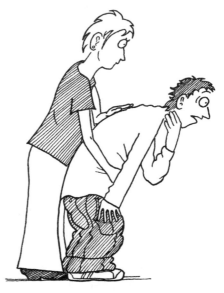

Give five sharp blows to the back in the area between the

shoulder blades. With luck, this will dislodge the object and it will come flying out of their mouth.

If this doesn't work, the next thing to try is some abdominal thrusts. To do this, you have to stand behind the person. Put both arms around the top part of their abdomen (stomach) just below the ribs. Clench your fist and hold this fist with your other hand. Pull upwards and inwards very quickly.

Again, this may dislodge the object. If it doesn't, you can try it again – up to five times. If this still doesn't work, go back to the back blows and keep on alternating five back blows with five abdominal thrusts.

If the person becomes unconscious, sometimes this causes the muscles to relax and an obstruction can pop out. Otherwise, you need to follow the resuscitation instructions on pages 179–182.

## Severe Bleeding

Even a small amount of bleeding can look alarming, so the first thing to remember is – don't panic! Most types of bleeding caused by accidents can be slowed or stopped while someone calls or goes for help. The best way of stopping the bleeding is to apply pressure, which controls the force of the blood flow and allows the blood to clot, 'gluing' the wound together.

If the injured part can be raised up above the level of the heart, this will slow down the blood flow to the wound. For example, if someone has a large cut on their leg after a fall off a bike, lie them down on the ground, lift up the leg and try to keep it supported about a metre above the ground.

Use a clean cloth pad if possible or, failing that, a wad of the cleanest part of your T-shirt, etc. and press it firmly over the bleeding area. If you have any cold water or ice, you can add that to the cloth because this helps to stop bleeding and decrease swelling.

Press firmly on the pad and the wound beneath for ten minutes. This will seem like a long time and you have to use a lot of pressure – but it should work.

If the bleeding is caused by a knife or something else sticking into the person, do not attempt to remove it.

Do not be tempted to give someone who has been unconscious or had a bad injury a drink, even water, and especially not a 'nice cup of sweet tea for the shock'. They may need an anaesthetic so that they can be stitched up or have broken bones set – and this must be given on an empty stomach.

### Burns or Electric Shock

If someone has been burned or suffered an electric shock, your first priority is to **safely** remove them from the danger area (see safety point below). If electricity is involved, e.g. they've been electrocuted by a faulty household appliance, turn it off at the mains first. If necessary, use something like a **non-metal** chair, broom or anything else that comes to hand, **as long as it is not metal**, to push or pull the injured person clear of danger.

**SAFETY POINT**

Items made of metal will conduct electricity, so you too could be electrocuted.

If you have to move someone who has been electrocuted, protect yourself by using something made of plastic or wood or rubber-coated – or, if available, put on thick rubber gloves.

If the environment is damp or wet, the above advice may also be unsafe – water is another conductor of electricity.

Call for help immediately. When you ring 999, the operator will ask you whether you need the fire brigade as well as an ambulance.

When somebody has been burned, the heat carries on damaging their flesh even after the source of the burn has been removed. Cooling down the flesh can help prevent this, so while you are waiting for help, try to soak the burned areas in cold water.

**Do not use ice.**

**Do not try to remove any stuck clothing.**

**Do not burst any blisters.**

With mild to moderate burns, the pain should start to die down after five minutes of water treatment. You can then allow the burn to dry naturally before covering it with a dry clean cloth if possible.

## *Suspected Meningitis*

Meningitis is a serious disease that can affect children and young adults and, on occasion, can kill within twenty-four to forty-eight hours. Early symptoms are similar to flu or any other viral illness, with the sufferer experiencing headache, shivering, high temperature and generally feeling unwell. The person with meningitis may have a severe headache, find it painful to bend their neck or complain that the light is hurting their eyes. None of these symptoms on their own definitely mean that someone has meningitis, but if they also have a dark, red, blotchy or mottled rash on any part of their body that does not fade when a glass is pressed against it, then you should get help immediately.

For more information on meningitis, see Chapter 6.

### Suspected Overdose or Alcohol Poisoning

An overdose of any kind of drug (legal, illegal or bought over the counter at the chemist's), including alcohol, may put someone's life in danger. Mixing any kind of drug with alcohol is particularly dangerous, especially if the person has a medical condition like epilepsy, diabetes or a heart problem. At first they may seem drowsy or confused and then fade into a deep sleep or unconsciousness. However, some drugs have the opposite effect, making the person anxious, overexcited and difficult to control. If you think someone has taken an overdose – either by accident or on purpose – you should get help immediately. In the meantime, try to keep them awake by tapping their shoulder and speaking loudly. Try to find out what they have taken and, if there are any remains of the drug or pill or medicine bottles around, gather them up to show the ambulance crew or doctor.

**Do not try to make them sick.**

## Jack's Story

Jack and his two best mates were fourteen. During the summer holidays they got really bored and started hanging around in the woods beyond the park moaning about their families and daring each other to do daft things. When it was Jack's turn for a dare, one of the other boys produced a bottle of gin he'd `borrowed' from somewhere and dared Jack to drink all of it. When he said he couldn't, the other two offered to help him out, but they'd already secretly decided that they wanted to get Jack completely drunk. It took most of the rest of the afternoon, and by the evening Jack was looking green and sweaty and the others were beginning to feel a bit worried. They tried to help him get up so they could drag him home, but his legs wouldn't move and he kept giggling and saying he was tired out and they should just leave him to sleep. They weren't feeling too brilliant themselves by this point, so they stumbled off to their own homes. They both meant to tell their parents what had happened but also realised they'd probably get into trouble. They assumed Jack would probably just wake up on his own and be OK. But a couple of hours later, Jack's mum started ringing round asking if anyone had seen him. Lots of questions were asked, and both boys looked so guilty that their own mums dragged the truth out of them. By the time his parents found Jack, he was completely unconscious, lying in a ditch freezing cold and barely breathing. They called an ambulance and he spent two days in hospital. He needed a drip to rehydrate him, and he didn't wake up at all for the first twenty-four hours. His parents were told that if he had not been found for another four hours he would have died from alcohol poisoning and the effects of the cold.

Strangely enough, none of the boys can even bear the smell of gin now!

*Jack, 14*

# Common Symptoms –
# What to Do and When to Get Help

The following are all common symptoms that most people experience at one time or another. Common sense will usually tell you when something is bad enough to ask for real medical help but, particularly when you are on your own and not feeling well, or when it is affecting someone close to you, it can be hard to remember what practical steps you can take to make things better.

## *Pain*

Pain is always a warning sign that something is wrong, yet everyone has had headaches or aches and pains that last for an hour or so and then go away. You are the best judge of what is normal for you. Mild headaches or muscular aches will usually respond to over-the-counter pain remedies like paracetamol or ibuprofen. Remember never to mix drugs and always to read the label, particularly the dosage information, carefully. However, if pain is severe, has no obvious cause like a bruise, sprain or other injury and doesn't go away after a couple of days, you should make an appointment to see your doctor.

### COMMON INJURIES FROM A TRIP OR FALL WHILE RUNNING OR PLAYING SPORT

These can be surprisingly painful, and joints like ankles, knees and wrists are particularly vulnerable. A general rule is that if you can move the joint or put any weight on it, then, while it may hurt a lot, it is unlikely to be broken. Self-treatment with RICE (see below) will usually be enough. If you are in any doubt, see your doctor or the Accident and Emergency department at your local hospital.

### RICE

RICE is the recommended treatment for a sprain or strain to any part of the body. It stands for:

- **R**est the affected part by keeping it still and avoiding putting weight on it.
- **I**cepacks or packs of frozen peas wrapped in a teacloth or T-shirt held against the injury for ten minutes every hour can help reduce swelling and pain.
- **C**ompression from a crêpe bandage or elasticated sports

support will also help keep swelling down – but always remove it before you go to bed.

- Elevation, i.e. propping up the injured joint on cushions or a sofa, will help drain fluid from the strain or sprain and reduce swelling.

### High Temperature (Fever)

Normal body temperature is around 37°C, although this can vary from person to person. A higher temperature is usually a sign that the body is trying to fight some kind of infection – anything from a simple sore throat bug to life-threatening meningitis.

Having a raised temperature can make you feel tired, headachy and generally miserable. Lying down and trying to get some rest is often a good idea. However, if the temperature goes too high, particularly in a young child, there is a risk of it affecting the brain, resulting in fits or convulsions. Sometimes with a high temperature, you start having very vivid dreams or even imagining things or voices when you're awake. This is a sign that the heat is affecting your brain and a warning that you need help to get the temperature down again. Although it is scary and unpleasant, there should be no lasting effect.

In a young person or adult, a temperature of 39°C (102°F if you have an old thermometer) or more should be considered a high fever. This isn't necessarily dangerous, but it is uncomfortable and can be frightening if you are on your own. Paracetamol can help to bring down a temperature – always check the dose on the label. Someone with a high temperature may feel shivery and cold in themselves, although their skin is hot to touch. Don't be tempted to wrap them up too much, as this may make them overheat – the cold shivery spells usually alternate with times when they start to feel hot. If you are looking after a friend with a temperature, try to cool them down by sponging them with tepid or lukewarm (not cold) water, or persuade them to have a cool (not cold) bath or shower. Use a fan or an open window to keep the air moving around them.

A high temperature can quickly make you dehydrated, so it's important to keep drinking, even if it's only sips of cold water or weak juice. Usually, a mixture of paracetamol, sponging and cold drinks will help bring down the temperature, but if it stays over 39°C for more than a day and you have other symptoms, you should get medical advice.

### Flu, Colds, Other Viruses and Antibiotics

Colds, flu and many other annoying but short-term illnesses are caused by viral infections. These are often passed on by coughs and sneezes. So if you have a streaming cold or think you're going down with feverish flu, you'll do everyone a favour by staying at home for a couple of days. Having some extra sleep and drinking plenty of cool drinks will make you feel better and allow your body to fight off the infection on its own. It might also prevent you from passing it on to everyone on the bus and at school.

Some people rush to see their doctor as soon as they feel a cold or flu coming on. This is rarely necessary, as viral infections do not respond to antibiotics and will usually get better within five to seven days whether or not you take any medication.

For coughs, colds and flu, try treating yourself first!

### Vomiting and/or Diarrhoea

Vomiting (being sick) and diarrhoea (loose bowels or 'having the runs') are very common and often the result of mild or serious food poisoning or the side-effect of another illness. Usually, they cure themselves in that they help the body get rid of whatever was causing the problem. But in the meantime they can make you feel lousy, and there's a risk that you can become quickly dehydrated through loss of fluid.

Anyone who feels nauseous or sick is usually better lying down. A cold wet cloth on their forehead or the back of their neck can help a lot. Although feeling sick is a horrid sensation, you often feel better once you have thrown up, but, unpleasant as it may be, you should always look to check that there is no blood (usually very dark red fluid streaks, or like dark coffee grounds) in the vomit. This is a sign of an emergency and you should get help at once.

When the body becomes dehydrated, it needs salts and sugars as well as water, so if you have had symptoms for several days it is important to replace these substances as well as to increase your fluid intake. You can buy special oral rehydration mixes in fizzy tablets or sachets from a pharmacy and some supermarkets, or you can make your own with four teaspoonfuls of sugar and a pinch of salt to half a litre of boiled or bottled water. Sweet fizzy drinks (like lemonade or cola) that have been allowed to go flat and then had a small pinch of salt stirred in can also be useful. Don't let someone who is feeling sick gulp a drink, as it will only make them worse, but encourage them to take small regular sips.

Nausea caused by **travel sickness** can often be prevented by over-the-counter pills from your pharmacist. Again, make sure you read the label and don't take more than the suggested dose – some of the tablets can make you feel very drowsy and a bit spaced out.

Ginger – in the form of ginger biscuits, crystallised ginger or tea made from slices of fresh ginger root – can also help.

You can buy special wrist bands from pharmacies and the travel supplies section of large supermarkets. These press on acupuncture points and seem to work very well for some people.

If travel sickness is a big problem for you, always try to travel in the front seat of the car or the front of a bus, make sure a window is open and never, ever try to read a book or even the map. You should look straight out at the road in front of you – don't turn around to talk to friends or look out of the side windows. Many people find that when they start driving themselves the travel sickness completely disappears.

**Pills for diarrhoea** – e.g. Immodium – are also available from a pharmacy or some supermarkets and can be very useful, particularly if you have to travel or carry on doing something while you have diarrhoea. But in general it's better to let your body get whatever is causing the problem out of your system first. Only take these medicines when absolutely necessary, as they can cause quite serious side-effects in a few people.

Most types of vomiting and diarrhoeal illnesses get better after a day or so but, if you are still ill after forty-eight hours you should seek medical advice.

## David's Story

I managed to get food poisoning on a walking and camping holiday with my friend. We'd planned the trip for ages and it was something to look forward to after exams. The first couple of days were fine, and I have to admit that we did have a few beers in the tent in the evening. The next morning I woke up feeling rough and thought it was just a hangover, but it just got worse and worse until I was throwing up and dashing into the bushes with diarrhoea every few minutes. I couldn't go on, but we were miles from anywhere, so we just put the tent up and decided to rest up overnight. I couldn't face food, and there wasn't anything else in me to come out, so I felt really weak. My friend has done lots of hiking and reads survival books and stuff, and he said it was important I should drink something and try to get some salt and sugar back into my body. He had half a bottle of cola in his rucksack and he opened it to let the fizz out. Then he put in a pinch of salt and swirled it around and made me take a sip every few minutes. I couldn't actually taste the salt at all, and he said that was because my body must have needed it. Although I didn't feel like drinking, I did keep trying and once I'd finished it all and rested up for a bit I felt much better and stronger.

*David, 17*

## Cuts and Bleeding

Minor cuts and bleeding are best treated by washing the wound in cold, running water. This helps clean it, and the cold also encourages the blood to clot, stopping the bleeding. If this does not work, apply pressure with a clean pad for about five to ten minutes or until the bleeding stops and then apply a sterile adhesive dressing or sticking plaster. For more severe bleeding, see Emergency Situations earlier in this chapter.

If you have a cut that is obviously dirty – e.g. a graze caused by sliding along a concrete surface – then you should bathe the wound in an antiseptic solution and try to remove any bits of grit. Really extensive wounds should be cleaned up in hospital. Everyone should make sure that they are up to date with their tetanus jabs. Tetanus is a very rare but extremely nasty bug that grows in the soil. If it gets into a wound, it can rapidly cause a severe infection, which can spread and affect the whole body – causing paralysis and even death in some people. Between the ages of fourteen and sixteen you should have your last dose of tetanus vaccination as part of your 'adolescent immunisations'. In most areas these are offered by your GP, although in a few places they are given at school.

# Matt's Story

Matt was a fantastic rugby player – playing for the school under-sixteen team and also playing for his local town. He was in a really tricky tackle and was gouged in the hand by one of the opponent's boots. His coach said he ought to go to the casualty department to get someone to check his wound out and to make sure he hadn't broken any bones in his hand, but he was more interested in going out for a beer after the game – he was so tall he didn't have any problems getting into the local pub. At first his hand seemed to be getting better, but about three days later he woke up and found that the whole of the back of his hand was puffy, and there was a red line going up his wrist and reaching almost to the elbow. He felt a bit shivery and sick, and realised he needed to get some advice. After a long wait in the hospital A and E department, he saw a doctor who explained that the wound had become infected and it would have to be explored. This meant an operation and an anaesthetic. Matt ended up with a big scar on his hand and was off rugby for the rest of the season. The doctors said that there were 20 millilitres (about a tablespoon) of pus in the wound, and the poison had started to track up towards the elbow. So Matt was on an antibiotic drip for forty-eight hours and then had to take more antibiotics at home. Luckily, he was up to date with his tetanus jabs, so he was very unlikely to get tetanus, but he was given a shot of special anti-tetanus serum just in case.

## *Earache*

You probably already know whether you're the type of person who gets earache a lot and, if so, may have your own ways of dealing with it. It is often linked with colds or sinus problems and may be caused by narrowing of the Eustachian tubes, which link the ears to the back of the throat. These are usually very flexible, allowing air to pass up and down, but they can become partially or fully blocked after a cold, or sinus or throat infection. Flying can also affect them.

Chewing, swallowing, sipping hot drinks and breathing steam (e.g. over a bowl of hot water or having a long hot bath or shower), or holding a hot-water bottle or a hot flannel next to the ear can all help relieve the blockage and reduce the earache. Your doctor may also suggest using nasal decongestants in the form of sprays or tablets to help reduce the discomfort. However, you may develop a severe ear infection that won't respond to any of these treatments, so if the pain continues you should see a doctor for further treatment.

### Sleepiness and Difficulty Waking

Most teenagers sleep a lot – usually at times when their parents would prefer them to be awake! But sometimes serious illness, alcohol or drugs can make someone particularly sleepy and hard to rouse. Sadly, this sometimes happens at sleepovers or when young people are away on holiday for their first time together without adults, and it can be very dangerous. If you can't wake someone by gently shaking their shoulder and speaking loudly to them, and particularly if you suspect that they have been drinking or taking any kind of drug – legal, illegal or over-the-counter – then you should get medical help. See also *Suspected Overdose or Alcohol Poisoning* earlier in this chapter.

# The 'Better-Than-Anything-You-Can-Ever-Buy-Ready-Made' First-Aid Kit

If all goes well, you won't have to use this kit. But when you start travelling on your own or just staying at home looking after your kid brother and sister, it can be reassuring to know you have a 'ready-for-everything' first-aid kit to hand and know how to use it.

It's very easy to spend large amounts of money on ready made kits, but many of these contain lots of plasters and bandages but very little for other common ailments. You'd do much better either to start from scratch or to buy something basic then add a few useful bits and pieces.

Everything listed below can be packed in a small make-up or toilet bag, which can then sit in your bathroom cabinet or fit in the bottom of your rucksack, ready to be whipped out if disaster strikes.

### Essential Items – Available from Pharmacies and Supermarkets

**Antiseptic:** It is important to wash wounds with clean water (boiled or bottled where possible) and use an antiseptic preparation to kill off any germs. A few individually packed antiseptic wipes can be useful, but a small bottle of liquid antiseptic can be diluted as necessary and used to wash out wounds before you apply a clean dressing.

**Sticking plasters:** Most packs contain far too many small ones and not enough larger plasters. It is much better to buy a strip of sticking plaster and keep it with a small pair of scissors. You can then cut off small strips for blisters, etc. and larger ones for cut knees and other injuries. A small roll of surgical tape can also be useful.

**Wound dressings:** A few sterile packs of individual non-stick wound dressings can be used to apply pressure to a bleeding wound and cover any kind of sore or injury. Make sure you take a selection of sizes. Use strips of surgical tape to hold them in place.

**Skin closure strips:** e.g. Steristrips. These come in a small packet and are tiny strips of almost transparent adhesive tape that are used to pull the edges of a wound together rather like stitches. They're very light to carry, take up hardly any space but, when you need them, you really need them!

**Crêpe bandage and safety pin:** Very useful for sprained ankles, wrists, etc.

**Antiseptic cream:** Small tube of antiseptic cream for soothing grazes, etc.

**Antihistamine or hydrocortisone cream:** Small tube for using (in small amounts) on itchy insect bites, sweat rashes, etc.

**Antihistamine tablets:** For minor allergic reactions.

**Small bottle of sterile eye drops:** Useful for easing sore and tired eyes or for flushing out foreign objects trapped under the eyelid.

**Motion sickness pills:** Hopefully, you'll never need them, but if you do you'll be glad they're there.

**Anti-diarrhoeals:** To be used if diarrhoea continues for more than a few hours and you have to keep moving or travelling.

**Oral rehydration mix:** Comes in sachets or tablets, but you can make your own if necessary. See *Vomiting and/or Diarrhoea* earlier in this chapter.

**Simple painkiller:** e.g. paracetamol or ibuprofen.

**Antacids:** in the form of tablets or chews. These help neutralise excess stomach acid caused by some foods or even alcohol.

**Small tin of petroleum jelly:** Petroleum jelly – such as Vaseline – is excellent for chapped lips, sore rubbed skin – and zips that stick!

And, if you are travelling, a tube of **insect repellent** and high-protection (SPF 15+) **sun cream**.

### Learning First Aid

If you have the opportunity to take a short first-aid course – in or out of school – then go for it. Failing that, get a simple book on first aid and read it. You really could save a life.

## Rosie's Story

I was going to see a film with some friends, and we had one of those bags of mixed sweets that we were all dipping into. Just as we walked up the stairs, my friend started coughing and choking. At first we thought she was mucking around, but then I saw that her face was going red and she was making clutching signs at her throat. She couldn't seem to speak at all, and I realised that her sweet had probably 'gone down the wrong way'. I looked around for help, but nobody seemed to be going to do anything, although lots of people were looking at her.

Then I remembered seeing a programme about first aid which said that you could unblock the throat of someone who was choking by pressing inwards and upwards under their ribs. I got behind her and put my arms around her, clasping my hands together in a fist, and tried to remember what I'd seen. I tugged my hands in hard, jerking up and under the front of her ribs. The first time I did it, nothing happened except she went quiet. But I did it again, harder this time, and the sweet shot out of her mouth across the floor. She was coughing and crying but she got her voice back and started thanking me. Everyone was really impressed, but I was just surprised. I hadn't even known that I'd remembered what to do until I had to do it.

Rosie, 14

# Personal Safety

The Suzy Lamplugh Trust is the UK's leading authority on personal safety. They provide advice leaflets and an excellent website at *www.suzylamplugh.org* (further details in Contacts section) and they have kindly allowed us to reproduce the following advice:

### Travelling on Foot
Many of us feel most vulnerable when on foot, but if you learn to recognise potential dangers you can usually avoid them.

- Avoid danger spots like quiet or badly lit alleyways, subways or isolated car parks. Walk down the middle of the pavement if the street is deserted.
- If you do have to pass danger spots, think about what you would do if you felt threatened. The best idea is to head for a public place where you know there will be other people, e.g. a garage or shop.

- If you are at all worried, try to walk with a friend or stay near a group of people.

- Avoid passing stationary cars with their engines running and people sitting in them.

- Try to keep both hands free and don't walk with your hands in your pockets.

- Always take the route you know best and try to use well-lit, busy streets.

- Walk facing oncoming traffic to avoid kerb crawlers.

- Stay aware of your surroundings – remember, if you are wearing a personal stereo you will not hear trouble approaching.

- It is a good idea to carry a mobile phone, a phonecard, or some spare change to enable you to make a phone call.

- Be careful when using cashpoint machines. Make sure nobody is hovering nearby and do not count your money in the middle of the street.

- If you think you are being followed, trust your instincts and take action. As confidently as you can, cross the road and turn and look to see who is behind you. If you are still being followed, keep moving. Make for a busy area and tell people what is happening. If necessary, call the police.

- If a vehicle pulls up suddenly alongside you, turn and walk in the other direction – you can turn much faster than a car.

- Beware of someone who warns you of the danger of walking alone and then offers to accompany you. This is a ploy some attackers have been known to use.

- Never accept a lift from a stranger or someone you don't know very well, even if you are wet, tired or running late.

- We all have the right to wear any clothes we wish, but we do need to consider the effect they may have on others. You can reduce risks by wearing clothes you can move in easily and shoes that fit well and are comfortable.

- Try not to keep all your valuables in one place. Instead, place items such as wallets in an inside pocket or use a money belt.
- One of the safest ways to carry things is in a small bag slung across your body under a jacket or coat. Ensure it sits close to your body.

### Travelling by Bus or Train

- Always wait for a bus or train in a well-lit place and near other people if possible.
- Try to sit near the driver or guard and make sure you can see as much of the bus deck or carriage as possible.
- Look for carriages on trains with lots of people in them. If a bus is not busy, stay on the lower deck.
- Notice where emergency alarms are located – there are alarms on every bus, in every train carriage and on every platform.
- Have your travel pass or correct change ready, so that your purse or wallet stays out of sight.
- Carry extra money in case you get stranded and need to take another bus or train or ring for a lift.
- Try to get someone to meet you if you are going to be alone when you get off at the bus stop or railway station.

### What to Do if You Feel Threatened

- If a situation makes you feel uneasy, you should try to get away at once. If you are on a bus or train, then move to a different seat or carriage. You can also alert the driver, guard or station staff.
- Don't panic. Breathe slowly and think clearly about how to react.
- Always give away your bag, purse or wallet rather than fighting to keep it. Your things can be replaced – you can't.
- Your voice is one of your best forms of defence. Don't be

embarrassed to make as much noise as possible to attract attention. Yell at the top of your voice, giving a specific instruction like, *'Phone the police!'*

- If you are on a bus or train, press the alarm. Railway platforms have telephones situated at the help points – it will connect you immediately to the British Transport Police or station staff.

- You could also phone 999. The operator will ask for your name, address and which emergency service you require. Give the information as clearly as you can and ask for the police. After you've contacted the emergency services, call your family and let them know where you are.

## Foreign Travel

You may be starting to dream of your first trip abroad without your parents – perhaps after exams or as part of a gap year. Obviously, different areas carry different risks, so the most important thing is to find out as much as you can before you go. The Foreign and Commonwealth Office offers excellent up-to-the-minute travel advice and tips at *www.fco.gov.uk*. However, the biggest dangers young travellers face are those of basic helath and sanitation.

For example, can you drink the water? Even some relatively developed places still have unreliable tap water, which tends to make unsuspecting visitors feel very ill. If in doubt, stick to bottled water which is cheaply available just about everywhere. Failing that, boil water before drinking it. And don't drink any drinks with ice in them! Don't forget that salads will probably have been washed in local water, so if you are unsure about the water supply steer clear of salads and fruit unless you peel it yourself. Food from local street markets can be very tempting, but make sure that anything you try has been well cooked, preferably while you watch.

The other thing to think about well in advance of any trip is whether or not you need any special vaccinations (such as for hepatitis, yellow fever, TB or cholera). Most vaccinations take about two weeks to become fully effective, and in some cases you need a course of vaccinations – it is no good thinking about this the day before you travel!

Be sure to find out if you need to take medicine to prevent you getting malaria. Each year, several gap students come back to England with this nasty parasite, and they can be ill for months with high fevers, headaches and sweating.

Various websites, including MASTA (see Contacts), give up-to-date health information and warnings for different countries.

But, finally, the biggest risk to young travellers is the totally unfounded belief that, just because they're on holiday, things will be safe. Not true! You're far more likely to be killed on a hired moped in Greece than in a plane crash on the way there. The local law may not require you to wear a helmet, but that doesn't mean you're safe without one.

### Don't Leave Your Common Sense at Home!

If you are planning on travelling around with friends – e.g. to celebrate the end of GCSEs – don't forget that, although you may think you are 'poor students', to many people you will seem very wealthy and you can easily become a target for attack. Try to stay with a couple of companions all the time, and don't be tempted to flash expensive cameras or phones around. Be respectful of the law and moral code in other countries, e.g. boys should keep T-shirts on if the local people object to seeing lots of bare flesh, and girls often need to cover up well, including knees and shoulders.

# 10 Getting Help and Helping Friends

**This chapter covers:**

- Why Do Some People Avoid Getting Help for a Problem?
- Choosing Someone to Turn To
- Helping a Friend

Most of this book has focused on things that can go wrong and what you can do about them. Hopefully, you'll realise that in nearly every case it's better to get help or (at least) find out more information about your problem. This chapter looks at the reasons why people might put off getting help and suggests different sources of support. A full list of helplines and sources of information can be found at the back of the book in the Contacts section.

## Why Do Some People Avoid Getting Help for a Problem?

Sometimes it's a lot easier to solve other people's problems than your own! What may seem obvious to you may be a depressing and paralysing muddle to your friend who is suffering from it. Seeking out and asking for help means taking action and requires courage. Luckily, most people find that once they've taken the first step they start to feel more in control of their life and better able to cope with whatever it is that's worrying them.

These are some of the reasons people put off seeking help:

**You may feel . . .** it isn't possible to get help for your particular problem.

**But, in fact . . .** most problems are solvable if you can find the right source of help, information or support.

**You may feel . . .** too embarrassed to admit to having this type of problem.

**But, in fact . . .** you are unlikely to be the first person ever to suffer from it. However, if you can't face talking to someone you know, or even speaking face to face with a doctor, you could try using a telephone or Internet helpline.

**You may feel . . .** that you can't trust anyone to keep what you say confidential.

**But, in fact . . .** doctors and most health workers have to keep what you tell them secret unless you give them specific permission to disclose it to anyone else. The only exception to this is if the doctor suspects you are being abused. If in doubt, you can ask them about this before you reveal anything personal. Or you can use a helpline, where you remain anonymous.

**You may feel . . .** scared that talking about your fear may somehow make it real, e.g. some people who are frightened they may have an illness like cancer have an almost superstitious fear that talking about the possibility could somehow make it come true.

**But, in fact . . .** it's in exactly these situations that you should get help as soon as possible. If you are seriously ill, early detection gives you a much greater chance of cure. And, if your problem isn't really serious, surely it's better to have your mind put at rest quickly rather than go on worrying unnecessarily?

**You may feel . . .** that you deserve to be ill or don't deserve to get help, e.g. you might worry that your illness is due to something you've done – drunk alcohol or taken drugs, say – or think that no one will take you seriously.

**But, in fact . . .** medical professionals and other helpers are very understanding about different lifestyles. The important thing is that someone wants to be helped. But feelings of 'not being worth helping' can also be a sign of depression. This could be a side-effect of an illness or a separate problem in itself. Either way, help is both possible and important.

**You may feel . . .** you don't want to admit to having the problem, because it's the sort of thing that 'only happens to other people'.

**But, in fact . . .** it could be your attitude that is half the problem. Admitting to a weakness or difficulty is the first step in overcoming it, but sometimes it takes a friend or an outsider to help you confront reality.

## Choosing Someone to Turn to

If you were injured or sick, you would obviously get help from a doctor or hospital – but not all situations are so straightforward. You may have a choice of people to turn to, so you will need to weigh up the advantages and disadvantages of each option. Your choice will be based on several factors, for example:

- how comfortable you feel talking to the other person;
- how much you think they can realistically help you;
- how much you trust them to keep any embarrassing or personal details confidential.

## Talking to Friends

This is often the obvious choice, because you're with them so much and you're used to discussing anything and everything with them.

**Advantages:** will probably be sympathetic and may have useful insights from having had similar problems themselves.

**Disadvantages:** they're unlikely to have much specialist knowledge and could be tempted to tell you what they think you want to hear rather than help you confront the truth. There may also be a risk they could gossip about your 'problem'.

## Talking to Parents or Carers

Parents or carers will probably consider themselves your first choice of someone to turn to, but, of course, sometimes they're part of the problem!

**Advantages:** they know you well and will almost certainly want to help, including being prepared to involve doctors or other specialist support as necessary. You can also rely on their long-term involvement – important if you're going through a difficult illness or suffering from depression.

**Disadvantages:** they may be a little too close to you! You could be scared of worrying them or letting them down or may feel that they would be judgemental or unsympathetic to your problem.

## Talking to Teachers or Other Adults

A favourite teacher or a friend's mum can be an excellent person to turn to, but you may want to pave the way before off-loading any major secrets on to them.

**Advantages:** they know you outside your home, so may have a more realistic idea of who you are and what you're about. They may have seen your problem before and, with teachers in particular, would probably know how to get you further help if necessary.

**Disadvantages:** they may feel they have to inform your parents – although this could be something you're grateful for! If you have a serious problem, they could find it hard to cope with the responsibility, so it's always best to ask someone first if you can confide in them and, if appropriate, check that they will feel comfortable about keeping what you say private and confidential.

### Talking to a Doctor or Health Worker

From the age of sixteen, anyone can change or choose their own GP but, even if you're younger than that, you can still usually make an appointment and see a doctor on your own.

**Advantages:** medical experts have access to specialist services if you need them. They should treat you as an adult and answer any questions you have. They can also put your mind at rest over many health worries. Everything you tell them will be confidential unless they have reasons to think you are at serious and immediate risk of harming yourself or others.

**Disadvantages:** going to see a doctor on your own can be daunting, particularly if you're really worried about something (taking along your mum or a friend can help). If you're nervous, you may find it difficult to ask questions, so writing them down beforehand and making a note of the answers can help. If you are in any doubt about this, you can ask for reassurance about confidentiality at the start of a session.

## Talking to a Helpline

Many different telephone and Internet helplines are available. You'll find a good selection in the Contacts section at the back of the book.

**Advantages:** any good helpline should have well-trained and experienced people available to answer your questions. You can remain anonymous and give only the information you feel comfortable sharing. Helpline counsellors understand how difficult it is to make that first call and should give you all the time you need.

**Disadvantages:** you don't know the person you're talking to. Sometimes the lines can be busy and it's hard to get through. The counsellors may not be able to give you the best help unless they know your full story and, most important, some helplines act as fronts for commercial, religious or political organisations. If the person at the other end sounds more interested in getting personal details or making you feel bad about yourself, make your excuses and hang up!

# Helping a Friend

If a friend confides a major worry, you may feel anxious yourself that you won't be able to do enough to help them. This is normal. The fact that they have already felt able to talk to you has been a help to them in itself. Listening and being sympathetic is very important, but for serious problems it's even more important to encourage your friend to get further help themselves. Remember one thing: if your friend has already told you about the problem, it means they are looking for help and may need you to take that step for them.

You can do this in several ways, for example:

- give them details of an appropriate helpline or information service (see Contacts);
- offer to be with them when they make the call or connection;
- suggest they consult a trusted teacher or another adult and again offer to be beside them or waiting outside the room to give support;
- encourage them to talk to their parents or carers – or to yours.

Often, doing one or more of the above will help your friend to take the next step. But sometimes, usually for one of the reasons listed at the beginning of the chapter, they won't want to do it. In that case you have a difficult decision to make. If you think your friend is at risk or in danger, you must do something yourself. You can give them an ultimatum and say that if they won't get help you will be forced to tell an adult for them. They won't be pleased, and they may even be angry with you, but if you care for them you must be prepared to get tough and do what you know is necessary. If in any doubt, you may want to call a helpline yourself.

The hardest thing to deal with is the friend who won't admit that there is a problem. Encouraging them to talk by being sympathetic and non-judgemental may help them open up. But, even if they don't, you may feel unable to cope with the worry you feel for them. In this case you both need help and support. You must accept that you can't bear the burden on your own. Talk to a trusted adult about the problem, even if you keep your friend's name out of it for the time being. You also need to tell your friend how you feel in the hope that they will take some action themselves.

# Contacts

**Note:** Telephone numbers beginning with 080 or 0500 are free to call from a BT landline and won't show up on the phone bill. However, these calls aren't free from most mobiles and may appear on the bill. Numbers starting 0845 are charged at local (cheap) rates on BT landlines and mobiles wherever in the country you call from, but they'll be on the phone bill.

## *General Help and Counselling for Young People*

### ChildLine
0800 1111
www.childline.org.uk
24-hour free, confidential helpline for young people with any problems

### ChildLine Eire (run by ISPCC)
Ireland Freephone 1800 666 666
www.ispcc.ie/childline.html

### Get Connected
0808 808 4994
www.getconnected.org.uk
Will direct you to the best service to help, whatever the problem. Open 1pm–11pm daily

### It's Not Your Fault
www.itsnotyourfault.org
Information and support for anyone going through a family break-up

### Samaritans
08457 90 90 90 (UK)
1850 90 90 90 (Eire)
www.samaritans.org
e-mail: jo@samaritans.org
24-hour confidential helpline for people with any problems

### There4me
www.there4me.com
Excellent website run by the NSPCC. Offers lots of useful information,

problem pages on many different subjects, one-to-one confidential consultations with on-line counsellors and links to many other good resources

**The Site**
020 7226 8008
www.thesite.org.uk
Lots of advice for 16- to 25-year-olds on all aspects of life

**Skill**
0800 328 5050
www.skill.org.uk
The National Bureau for Students with Disabilities

**Muslim Women's Helpline**
020 8904 8193 and 020 8908 6715
www.mwhl.org

## Mental Health Issues

**@ease**
020 8974 6814
www.rethink.org.at-ease
E-mail for confidential advice about mental health: advice@rethink.org
Web-based mental health resource for young people under stress or with worries about their thoughts and feelings. @ease is part of Rethink, the severe mental health organisation. Open 10am–3pm weekdays.

**Depression Alliance**
020 7633 0557
www.depressionalliance.org.uk
Information and support on all aspects of depressive illness

**No Panic**
0808 808 0545
www.nopanic.org.uk
Information and support for panic attacks, phobias, obsessive-compulsive disorders (OCDs). Open 10am–10pm daily

**Young Minds**
www.youngminds.org
National charity committed to improving the mental health of all children and young people. Offers excellent downloadable information for young people

**Read the Signs**

www.readthesigns.org

Department of Health site covering signs of mental distress, including self-harm. Very good information for young people

## Sexual Health Issues

**Brook**

0800 0185 023

www.brook.org.uk

Provides free, confidential contraception and sex advice for young people under twenty-five. Open 9am–5pm weekdays

**Family Planning Association**

0845 310 1334

www.fpa.org.uk

Medical advice on contraception, pregnancy and STIs. Open 9am–6pm weekdays

**Lesbian and Gay Switchboard**

020 7837 7324 (phone for referral to local centres, or check phone book)

www.llgs.org.uk

**Sexwise**

0800 28 29 30

www.ruthinking.co.uk

Free advice and information on sex and relationships for under-18s. Open 7am–12am

**For more information on puberty and growing up**

www.wiredforhealth.gov.uk

www.mindbodysoul.gov.uk

## HIV and AIDS

**Avert**

www.avert.org.uk

E-mail: info@avert.org.uk

**Sexual Healthline** (formerly the National AIDS Helpline)
0800 567 123
www.playingsafely.co.uk

**Terrence Higgins Trust**
0845 12 21 200
www.tht.org.uk
Open 10am –10pm weekdays, 12pm–6pm weekends

## Health Issues

**NHS Direct**
0845 4647
www.nhsdirect.nhs.uk
Free helpline for medical queries and advice on whether or not a symptom
is a medical emergency. Open 24 hours

**Acne Support Group**
0870 870 2263
www.stopspots.org
Advice and support for people suffering from acne

**Eating Disorders Association**
0845 634 7650. 18-year-olds and under. Open 4pm–6.30pm weekdays
0845 634 1414. Adult helpline. Open 8.30am–8.30pm weekdays
www.edauk.com
Support and advice for anyone experiencing difficulties with eating

**Embarrassing Problems**
www.embarrassingproblems.com
Site offering advice on embarrassing problems, e.g. wind

**ME Association**
www.meassociation.org.uk
A membership organisation for people affected by ME. Free membership to
under-eighteens

**Meningitis Research Foundation**
0808 800 3344.(UK)
1890 41 33 44 (Eire)
www.meningitis.org

Offers clear information on symptoms of meningitis and septicaemia. Open 24 hours

**National Society for Epilepsy**
01494 601400
www.epilepsynse.org.uk
UK epilepsy helpline. Open 10am–4pm, weekdays

**Toast**
01279 866010
www.toast-uk.org.uk
The Obesity Awareness & Solutions Trust

## Bullying

**Anti-Bullying Campaign**
020 7378 1446
www.bullying.co.uk
E-mail: help@bullying.co.uk
Advice for victims of bullying. Open 10am–4pm weekdays

## Young People in Care or Away From Home

**Message Home**
0800 700 740 (over 18)
www.missingpersons.org
Confidential contact/message service offered by the National Missing Persons Helpline

**Who Cares? Trust**
LinkLine 0500 564 570
www.rhrn.thewhocarestrust.org.uk
Support and advice for young people in care. Open 3.30pm–6pm Mon, Wed, Thur

## Personal Safety

**The Suzy Lamplugh Trust**
020 8876 0305
www.suzylamplugh.org

## *Support for Victims of Crime and Abuse*

### Rape Crisis Centres
London 020 7837 1600 (phone for referral to local centres, or check phone book)
www.rapecrisis.co.uk
E-mail: info@rapecrisis.org.uk

### Survivors UK
0845 122 1201
www.survivorsuk.org.uk
Advice and support for young men who have been victims of sexual abuse or male rape. Open 7pm–10pm Tue, Thur

### Victim Support
0845 30 30 900
www.victimsupport.org
National charity for people affected by crime, offering free and confidential support to help victims deal with the experience, whether or not the crime is reported. Open 9am–9pm weekdays, 9am–7pm weekends

## *Bereavement*

### Compassionate Friends
08451 23 23 04 www.tcf.org.uk
Offers support to all families bereaved after the death of a child or children. Helpline open 10am–4pm, 6.30pm–10.30pm daily.

### Cruse Bereavement Care
0870 167 1677
www.crusebereavementcare.org.uk
E-mail: helpline@crusebereavementcare.org.uk
Advice and counselling for anyone who has been affected by a death. Open 3pm–6pm Mon, Wed, Fri

## *Legal Advice for Young People*

### Children's Legal Centre
01206 873 820
www.childrenslegalcentre.com

E-mail: clc@essex.ac.uk
Open 10am–12.30pm, 2pm–4.30pm weekdays

**National Youth Advocacy Service**
0800 616 101
www.nyas.net
NYAS offers advice, information, support and representation to any child or young person who wants to have their wishes and feelings taken into account when decisions are made about them

## *Addictions*

**Alateen**
020 7403 0888
www.al-anonuk.org.uk
Advice for young people whose lives have been affected by someone else's problem with alcohol. Open 10am–4pm daily

**Drinkline**
0800 917 8282
Advice on alcohol problems. Open 7am–11pm weekdays, and 24 hours (from 9am Friday to 11pm Monday)

**Wrecked**
www.wrecked.co.uk
Information and advice on alcohol problems

**FRANK** (formerly the **National Drugs Helpline**)
0800 776600
www.talktofrank.com
24-hour confidential advice, information and support to anyone concerned about drug misuse

**Gamcare**
0845 6000 133
www.gamcare.org.uk
Committed to promoting responsible attitudes to gambling and the provision of proper care for those who have been harmed by gambling dependency

**Quit**
0800 002200

www.quit.org.uk
E-mail: stopsmoking@quit.org.uk
Free help and information on how to stop smoking. Open 9am–9pm daily

**Release**
0845 4500 215
www.release.org.uk
E-mail: ask@release.org.uk
Drugs information and legal advice charity

**Re-solv**
0808 800 2345
www.re-solv.org.
E-mail: helpline@re-solv.org
The Society for the Prevention of Solvent and Volatile Substance Abuse.
Open 9am–5pm weekdays

## First-Aid Training

**British Red Cross**
www.redcross.org.uk

**Duke of Edinburgh's Award Scheme** (often offered/required within the
award training)
www.theaward.org

**St John Ambulance**
08700 10 49 50
www.sja.org.uk

## Advice for Travellers

**Foreign and Commonwealth Office**
www.fco.gov.uk
Offers up-to-the-minute advice and tips for travellers for anywhere you
might possibly visit

**MASTA**
0113 238 7575
www.masta.org
For travel and health advice

## *Contacts for Parents*

### It's Not Your Fault

www.itsnotyourfault.org.uk

Offers information and support to both young people and parents over separation and divorce

### Papyrus

01706 214449

www.papyrus-uk.org/papyrus-help-for-parents.html

Charity committed to the prevention of young suicide and the promotion of mental health and emotional well-being

### ParentLine Plus

0808 800 2222

www.parentlineplus.org.uk

Help and information for anyone involved in caring for children and young people, with specific sections for families breaking up and step-families

### SaneLine

0845 767 8000

www.sane.org.uk

Advice and support for the sufferers of mental illness and their families. Open 12pm–2am daily

### Trust for the Study of Adolescence

01273 693311

www.tsa.uk.com

E-mail: info@tsa.uk.com

Provides information and resources for professionals working with adolescents and parents

### Young Minds

0800 018 2138

www.youngminds.org.uk

The Parents' Information Service. Open 10am–1pm Mon, Fri, 1pm–4pm Tues, Wed, Thur

### e-parents

www.e-parents.org/pis

The National Families and Parenting Institute's website for parents

# Final Reminder - Emergency Situations Where You Must Get Help - FAST!

In some situations you don't have the luxury of time to worry about whether getting help is the right thing to do. If you don't take action immediately, you could be putting your own or someone else's life at risk.

Many of the situations described here are dealt with in more detail elsewhere in the book. If you or someone you are with has any of the following symptoms, they need to be seen by a doctor or taken to the Accident and Emergency department (casualty) of the local hospital – IMMEDIATELY.

### Temperature Above 40°

Having a high temperature is a sign that someone is seriously unwell – not a disease in itself. It may be due to a virus that you can't do much about, but it could mean a serious infection that requires immediate treatment. Common causes of really high temperatures in young people are:

- meningitis;
- pneumonia;
- kidney infection.

### Unconscious or Collapsed and Can't Be Woken

Common causes in young people are:

- the effects of too much alcohol – with or without drugs;
- following a head injury;
- a serious infection involving the brain (such as meningitis);

- a diabetic coma;
- a drugs overdose.

## Choking Leading to Cyanosis (Going Blue)

Usually, this is due to choking on food, but many young people also choke on vomit if they have been drinking alcohol and have become unconscious. The cyanosis means that not enough oxygen is getting into the bloodstream.

## A Rash That Doesn't Fade When a Glass Is Pressed Against It

This is the classic sign of a severe form of meningitis called meningococcal septicaemia.

## A Fit in Someone Who Isn't Known to Be Epileptic

This may be the first sign that they are going to develop epilepsy, but fits can also occur due to brain tumours or head injury.

## A Burn from an Electric Shock

There are two reasons for getting help quickly: firstly, the shock may have caused internal damage as well as the visible burn, and secondly the burn itself is often more serious than it looks at first.

## A Fracture With a Cut in the Skin Above It

This may happen after someone has been in a car crash, fallen off their bike or broken a leg or arm playing sport. If the skin is broken, the fracture is called a compound fracture. Germs can get into the bone quite quickly, and this can lead to a serious bone infection called osteomyelitis – which can take months to heal. If you are with someone who has this sort of fracture, get them to hospital straight away.

### Severe Abdominal Pain

This could mean appendicitis, which needs urgent treatment.

You may find that if you ring emergency services or go with someone to an A and E (casualty) department, the staff don't take you seriously at first if you are not an adult – but don't be put off. Stand your ground (but stay polite!) and insist that you are seen quickly. Tell the receptionist or the nurse who you meet first exactly what it is you are worried about. If you ring for an ambulance, speak very clearly, tell them how long the person has been ill, and describe their colour, how they are breathing, and whether the patient is able to talk to you. Make sure you give any directions slowly and clearly, as getting the ambulance there a few minutes more quickly really could help to save someone's life.

# Glossary

| | |
|---|---|
| Addiction | A craving and/or dependency on something that is psychologically or physically habit-forming. |
| AIDS | Stands for acquired immune deficiency syndrome. |
| Allergen | A substance to which someone has an allergy, e.g. peanuts, wasp stings, shellfish. |
| Anaemia | A condition where someone has too few red blood cells. This can make them pale, easily tired and breathless, as not enough oxygen is being carried around their body. |
| Anaphylaxis | A severe allergy. |
| Anorexia nervosa | A psychological illness where people believe they are too fat and starve themselves or use other methods, such as vomiting or taking laxatives, to lose weight. |
| Antibiotic | A drug used to treat infection caused by bacteria. |
| Anti-depressant | Drugs prescribed by a doctor or hospital that help combat depression. |
| Antiseptic | A chemical, usually a cream or solution, that can destroy or slow the growth of bacteria and viruses, which all cause disease. |
| Appendicitis | Inflammation (redness and swelling) of the appendix. |
| Asthma | A condition where the lining of the air passageways in the lungs becomes swollen and narrowed, causing shortness of breath and difficulty breathing. |
| Bipolar disorder | A serious type of depression, which can suddenly turn into an overexcited or manic phase. |
| Bone marrow | A spongy material found inside long bones, such as the thigh bone, which produces different types of blood cells. |
| Bone marrow transplant | An injection of cells taken from the inside of a donor's bone. This can allow the patient's body to make new, healthy white cells. |

| | |
|---|---|
| Bulimia nervosa | A condition where someone alternates overeating and undereating in order to maintain their weight at a certain level. This can be combined with vomiting or taking laxatives. |
| Chemotherapy | A drug treatment either taken orally or injected directly into the veins that targets cancerous cells. |
| Chlamydia | A common sexually transmitted infection (STI) which, if not treated, can lead to infertility in men and women. |
| Chronic Fatigue Syndrome (CFS) | See ME. |
| Cognitive-behaviour therapy (CBT) | A talking treatment that is very effective for anxiety-related disorders and depression. |
| Dehydration | Lack of water in the body tissues, due to insufficient intake or excess loss of water (e.g. by vomiting or diarrhoea). |
| Diabetes | Condition where the body has a problem dealing with sugar in the bloodstream. |
| Diarrhoea | Loose bowels or 'having the runs'. |
| Electro-cardiogram (ECG) | A recording of the electrical activity of the heart. |
| Electro-encephalogram (EEG) | A brain-wave test. |
| Epilepsy | A condition where someone has a series of seizures or fits caused by sudden outbursts of electro-chemical activity in one area of the brain. |
| Genital warts | Lumps, caused by the human papilloma virus, which occur in the genital area. |
| Glandular fever | An acute infection that affects the body's immune system. Also known as infectious mononucleosis. |
| GP | General practitioner or family doctor. |

| | |
|---|---|
| Grieving | A period of feeling very sad about the loss of a person or relationship. |
| GUM clinic | A specialist genito-urinary medicine clinic, also called a special clinic for sexually transmitted infections. |
| Hepatitis | An illness involving inflammation of the liver. |
| HIV | Human immunodeficiency virus. The virus that causes AIDS. |
| Hodgkin's disease | A malignant disease of the lymphatic tissue, usually involving swelling of the glands in the neck, armpits or groin. |
| Infectious mononucleosis | An acute infection that affects the body's immune system. Also known as glandular fever. |
| Insulin | A hormone produced by the pancreas gland that controls the sugar level in the blood. |
| Leukaemia | Cancer of the blood cells, which are produced in the bone marrow. |
| Lymph | Fluid that bathes the tissues – containing salts, water and protein and various types of white blood cells. |
| Lymph gland | A small swelling made of lymph tissue. Acts as a filter for lymph, and produces white cells, which help to fight infections. |
| Malignant | Something that does you harm. |
| Malignant melanoma | A dangerous form of skin cancer. |
| Manic depression | A serious type of depression that can suddenly turn into an overexcited or manic phase. |
| ME (myalgic encephalopathy) | A condition where someone experiences severe fatigue (tiredness) for at least six months. It is made worse by physical exercise and is usually associated with weak or painful muscles and poor concentration. |
| Meningitis | A serious infection usually caused by a virus or bacterium. Results in inflammation of the covering of the brain and spinal cord, making someone very ill very quickly. |

| | |
|---|---|
| Migraine | A severe headache, often with nausea, which can last up to two days. |
| Mortuary | A place for temporarily storing the dead. |
| Mourning | The process of coming to terms with the death of someone close to you. |
| Nausea | A feeling that you are about to vomit. |
| Neuro-surgery | Surgery carried out on the brain. |
| Nicotine | The addictive drug contained in tobacco |
| Obesity | Severely overweight. |
| Oesophagus | The tube that takes food from the mouth to the stomach. |
| Over-the-counter medication | Drugs that can be bought without a doctor's prescription. |
| Panic attack | The body's reaction to extreme anxiety. |
| Peer pressure | The feeling that you have to do what everyone else is doing. |
| Phobia | An irrational fear of something. |
| Platelets | A type of blood cell produced in the bone marrow that makes the blood sticky and helps it to clot so that bleeding can be controlled. |
| Post-mortem | Literally means 'after death', but a post-mortem examination is an investigation into the cause of death by examining the dead body. |
| Psychosis | A severe mental disorder that involves loss of contact with reality. Sufferers often have delusions and hallucinations. Schizophrenia and manic depression are types of psychotic disorders. |
| Post-viral fatigue syndrome (PVFS) | See ME. |
| Radiotherapy | Small doses of radiation aimed directly at a tumour to kill the cells. |
| Resuscitation | The process of bringing back to life someone who appears to be dead by restoring a heartbeat and breathing. |

| | |
|---|---|
| Rigor mortis | Stiffening of a dead body, several hours after death, caused by the release of natural chemicals in the body. |
| Schizophrenia | A severe mental disorder where someone cannot think clearly, has no understanding of reality and often has delusions and hallucinations. Patients often believe their thoughts are being controlled by someone else. |
| Seizure | A fit, usually due to epilepsy, where someone has odd shaking movements and/or becomes unconscious for a short period. |
| Surgery | An operation, usually under a general anaesthetic, i.e. while you're asleep. |
| Tonsillitis | Inflammation of the tonsils, usually caused by viral or bacterial infection. |
| Toxin | A poisonous substance. |
| Trachea | The windpipe or tube leading from the back of the mouth to the lungs. |
| Tumour | A growth, swelling or an enlargement. |
| Unconscious | Unaware of what is happening, not rousable when shaken or spoken to. |
| Undertaker | A person who usually works in a funeral home and who is responsible for dealing with dead bodies and organising the funeral. |
| Vaccination | A way of protecting someone from an illness by giving them a tiny amount of the virus or bacterium (in a changed form) that causes that illness. This makes the patient produce antibodies that will protect them if they are in contact with the real disease. |
| Virus | A tiny infectious particle that can grow in living cells. Viruses cause many common diseases, including chickenpox, mumps, measles, AIDS – and the common cold. Viruses do not respond to antibiotics. Some can be prevented by vaccination. |
| Vomiting | Throwing up or being sick. |

# Index

If you would like more information about books available from Piccadilly Press and how to order them, please contact us at:

Piccadilly Press Ltd.
5 Castle Road
London
NW1 8PR

Tel: 020 7267 4492
Fax: 020 7267 4493

Feel free to visit our website at
www.piccadillypress.co.uk